The China–Latin America Axis

The China–Latin America Axis

Emerging Markets and the Future of Globalisation

Gastón Fornés
University of Bristol (UK) and
ESIC Business & Marketing School (Spain)

and

Alan Butt Philip
University of Bath (UK)

palgrave
macmillan

First published 2012 by
PALGRAVE MACMILLAN

Palgrave Macmillan in the UK is an imprint of Macmillan Publishers Limited, registered in England, company number 785998, of Houndmills, Basingstoke, Hampshire RG21 6XS.

Palgrave Macmillan in the US is a division of St Martin's Press LLC, 175 Fifth Avenue, New York, NY 10010.

Palgrave Macmillan is the global academic imprint of the above companies and has companies and representatives throughout the world.

Palgrave® and Macmillan® are registered trademarks in the United States, the United Kingdom, Europe and other countries.

ISBN: 978–0–230–57487–8

This book is printed on paper suitable for recycling and made from fully managed and sustained forest sources. Logging, pulping and manufacturing processes are expected to conform to the environmental regulations of the country of origin.

A catalogue record for this book is available from the British Library.

A catalog record for this book is available from the Library of Congress.

10 9 8 7 6 5 4 3 2 1
21 20 19 18 17 16 15 14 13 12

Printed and bound in the United States of America

To my parents, an endless source of good examples and inspiration.

Gaston

To my teachers and my students, who continue to inspire me.

Alan

Contents

Tables

Figures

Boxes

Acknowledgements

First, we would like to thank the institutions that helped and supported us during the development of this book, in particular the University of Bath School of Management, ESIC Business and Marketing School, and SPAIS at the University of Bristol.

Second, we would like to express our gratitude to various people who in different ways have helped us during this process: Jose Duran from ECLAC, Luis Bussio from the China–Argentina Chamber of Commerce, Neil Davila from ProMexico, Xu Ning from Nanjing University, Ma Jikai from the Ningxia Foreign Experts Bureau, Angus MacInnes, and Luis Tapia from World Trade Center, San Luis Potosi and Anna Trueman.

We are also grateful for the assistance from several colleagues at the Technological University of Monterrey both in San Luis Potosi and at the CCM campus in Mexico City.

Finally, and most importantly, we would like to thank our families and friends for being patient and supportive while we wrote this book.

1
Introduction

> South America is going to be the hot spot for Chinese investment in the coming ten years... Entrepreneurs who want to 'challenge the blue ocean' should be ready to go to South America.
>
> Chen Yuan, President, China Development Bank[1]

1.1 Context and motivation

Since the 2004 visit of China's President, Hu Jintao, to Latin America, the growing relationship between the two regions has been appearing in the news across the world. This was the second visit of a president of the People's Republic of China to Latin American countries in the twentieth century and its consequences are still impacting the dynamics of the world economy. One of the most visible results of this visit is the explosion of trade between China and Latin America; by 2010 it had reached similar levels to those of the trade between the EU and Japan at the end of the 1990s, thus rivalling one of the traditional axes of the Triad.

This relationship, which has been growing at rates between 40%–50% per year during the last ten years, is also changing the shape of globalisation. Around 40% of the flows of foreign direct investment are going to China and Latin America (50% to emerging markets), companies from both regions are becoming relevant players in world markets, and for the first time since the publishing of the Brandt Report in 1980 a strong South–South trade axis is developing.

This relationship is also changing the political landscape of the world. China has become a powerful contestant to the United States' traditional influence in Latin America and, if the trend continues, it will replace the EU as the largest foreign investor in the region in the next few years. Latin America has also leveraged its position in the world stage by getting closer to China. It is now an important player in the G20, it has diminished its economic dependence on the United States and the EU, and its economy has posted above average growth in the last five to seven years.

This relationship has also been beneficial for both China and Latin America. On the one hand, Chinese companies have found in Latin American countries a growing middle class hungry to consume their low and medium priced manufactured goods. On the other hand, Latin American firms can sell their agricultural products (where they have clear competitive advantages) to the big Chinese market without the restrictions imposed by the EU and the United States. The financial crisis that started in 2007 has only increased these effects. China and Latin America have hardly felt the impact of the crisis and their economies have continued to grow at high rates, a situation completely different from what is currently seen in developed economies, in particular in the EU.

These events and changes were the main motivation to write this book. In this context it attempts to provide a deep, objective, and thorough analysis of the relationship between China and Latin America, including past and present events. It also presents the trends that are currently developing and discusses their possible consequences. It does this at three different levels: political, trade and investments, and companies. As this is a new phenomenon, the text highlights the trends to watch and proposes possible scenarios. In any case, it is clear from what is shown in this book that the world is going to a more balanced configuration in which the influence of the United States, the EU, and Japan is decreasing while the weight and importance of emerging markets is increasing. This is definitely shaping the future of globalisation.

1.2 Structure

The book is structured to present the relationship between China and Latin America from different perspectives. Chapter 2 introduces the China–Latin America axis within the context of emerging markets. This chapter analyses the growth and development of emerging markets in the last 20 years, their share in international trade and foreign investments, the main characteristics and features of their business environment, the local companies, and a section called 'Emerging Cities', which claims that these urban agglomerations are the real emerging markets. This chapter concludes by introducing China–Latin America as the emerging markets' axis and explains why this relationship is relevant in the context of globalisation.

Chapter 3 studies in detail the economic and commercial relations between China and Latin America. It starts by showing the political ties, and then presents an analysis of the trade and investment flows between the regions, followed by some perspectives for the next years. After this, the chapter introduces the main players: first it discusses Latin America as a continent, second, it provides a short history of nine Latin American countries, and third, it gives a short history of China. Chapter 3 concludes with a comparison between these markets and prospects for the future.

In Chapter 4 the analysis turns to the political side. The focus of this chapter is the benefits for both China and Latin America of this growing relationship in political, economic, and social terms. Some of the points discussed in this chapter are: the rivalry–partnership relationship between China and Latin America, the extent to which the growing relationship with China is beneficial to all Latin American countries, the potential threats to domestic producers posed by Chinese exports, and the possibilities for further economic integration in Latin America.

Then, Chapter 5 makes a thorough analysis of Chinese firms in Latin America. It first studies the main characteristics of these companies including drivers, facilitators, and stages of their international expansion; then it presents their current situation, an analysis of their capabilities, and prospects for the next years. It continues with a section on the Chinese dragons in Latin America where their operations in the region are analysed. The chapter discusses the fit of China's companies to the Latin American environment and also the strength of their capabilities in the low and medium technology sectors vis-à-vis the local competitors.

Chapter 6 continues with the analysis of companies, this time from Latin America. It presents the history and recent developments of multilatinas, their main characteristics and drivers for their expansion. There is a section in which the challenges faced by multilatinas in China are studied in detail. The chapter focuses on the industries in which companies from Latin America are doing well in China, and also on the psychic distance between the two regions, as the two regions are too diverse.

Finally, to provide an outsider's view, Chapter 7 analyses the China–Latin America axis from the perspective of the United States and the EU. This is relevant as both have traditionally been large investors in the region with strong political, social and historical ties. It also includes a section on the potential impact of China on the regional integration in Latin America. The chapter discusses the arrival of China in Latin America, which can be seen as a new source of 'soft imperial power', the possibility that China's bilateralism could undermine the efforts to strengthen regional integration and how the relationship with China is transforming the geopolitical landscape of Latin America. Chapter 8 presents the conclusions of the book.

2

Emerging Markets: The Markets of the Future

> Global institutions had failed to fully reflect the changing status of developing countries in the world economy and finance.
>
> Hu Jintao, China's President[1]

2.1 Introduction

Emerging markets have been appearing increasingly in the media, specialised literature and MNEs annual reports in the last 15 to 20 years. During this period, acronyms like BRIC (Brazil, Russia, India, China), BRICET (BRIC + Eastern Europe + Turkey), BRICS (BRIC + South Africa), VISTA (Vietnam, Indonesia, South Africa, Turkey, Argentina), BRICM (BRIC + Mexico), BRICK (BRIC + South Korea), CIVIETS (Colombia, Indonesia, Vietnam, Egypt, Turkey and South Africa), or Next Eleven (Bangladesh, Egypt, Indonesia, Iran, Mexico, Nigeria, Pakistan, Philippines, South Korea, Turkey and Vietnam) were coined and are now common in the business vocabulary. Also during this period, ten transition economies from Eastern Europe joined the European Union (EU) and from them five entered the Eurozone. Emerging markets have also increased their weight in political terms in recent years as the Group of Twenty (G20)[2] has replaced the Group of Eight (G8) to 'become the new permanent council for international economic cooperation' (CNN.com, 2009). However, along with the many acronyms, there are various definitions of emerging markets as well as different lists of these markets.

2.2 Emerging markets

Until the end of the 1970s, 'less economically developed countries' (LEDCs), based on objective or subjective indicators, was the common term for countries that were less developed in comparison with the United States, Western Europe or Japan. This term carried the idea of high potential for profits but with higher risks. The term was thought not positive enough and as a consequence the label 'emerging market' appeared and since then it has been used with 'emerging economies' interchangeably.

The term 'emerging markets' 'was coined, the literature seems to agree, in the early 1980s by Antoine van Agtmael, then working for the World Bank's International Financial Corporation. The phrase was defined in terms of economics and levels of wealth. Emerging markets were economies with low-to-middle per capita income. It quickly came to be understood that emerging markets also needed to boost their growth, open their markets, and embark on structural reform. For years, the term was synonymous with the Asian tiger economies' (Authers, 2006).

At the beginning of the 2000s, new definitions and lists appeared in specialised literature. For example, Arnold and Quelch (1998) said that emerging markets are countries that satisfy at least two criteria: (1) a rapid pace of economic development, and (2) government policies favouring economic liberalisation and the adoption of a free-market system. At that time, the International Financial Corporation (IFC, 1999) identified 51 rapidly growing countries in Latin America, Africa, Asia and the Middle East as emerging economies and to this Hoskisson, Eden, Lau and Wright (2000) added 13 transition economies from the list of the European Bank for Reconstruction and Development (European Bank for Reconstruction and Development, 1998). This made a total of 64 emerging markets at the beginning of the twenty-first century.

After this, in 2001, Goldman Sachs' chief economist Jim O'Neill developed the idea of BRICs to indicate the countries he expected to be the next to enter the economic big league. He said that the BRICs, Korea and Mexico 'should not be really thought of as "emerging markets" in the classical sense, as many still do. We regard these countries as a critical part of the modern globalised economy'.[3]

With these definitions issues appeared when analysis and comparisons were attempted. These economies are too diverse; the pace and depth of their political and economic changes, and the size of their markets are only examples of the differences. Is it possible to have in the same group countries like Argentina, Pakistan and Lithuania; or China, Trinidad, Tobago and Jordan? For this reason, probably, *The Economist* (2008) proposed to retire the phrase 'emerging markets' and supported the more rigorous three categories recently published by the FTSE group based on the development levels of local stock markets[4]: (1) advanced emerging, (2) secondary emerging and (3) frontier markets. Table 2.1 shows the list of countries in each category as of September 2010.

Table 2.1 FTSE Global Equity Index Series

Developed	Advanced emerging	Secondary emerging	Frontier markets
Australia	Brazil	Chile	Argentina
Austria	Hungary	China	Bahrain
Belgium/ Luxembourg	Mexico	Colombia	Bangladesh
Canada	Poland	Czech Republic*	Botswana
Denmark	South Africa	Egypt	Bulgaria
Finland	Taiwan	India	Côte d'Ivoire
France		Indonesia	Croatia
Germany		Malaysia*	Cyprus
Greece		Morocco	Estonia
Hong Kong		Pakistan	Jordan
Ireland		Peru	Kenya
Israel		Philippines	Lithuania
Italy		Russia	Macedonia
Japan		Thailand	Malta
Netherlands		Turkey*	Mauritius
New Zealand		UAE	Nigeria
Norway			Oman
Portugal			Qatar
Singapore			Romania
South Korea			Serbia
Spain			Slovakia
Sweden			Slovenia
Switzerland			Sri Lanka
UK			Tunisia
United States			Vietnam

Note: *Czech Republic, Malaysia and Turkey will be promoted to advanced emerging market status beginning in June 2011.
Source: FTSE, 2010.

Box 2.1 FTSE Emerging Markets Index performance compared to FTSE All World Index

Figure 2.1 shows the performance for the FTSE Emerging Markets Index[5] compared with the FTSE All World Index from January 2006 to January 2011. In this figure, it is possible to see that the Emerging Markets Index has outperformed the All World Index over the period of analysis; this is particularly relevant as the period was dominated by a deep economic and financial crisis.

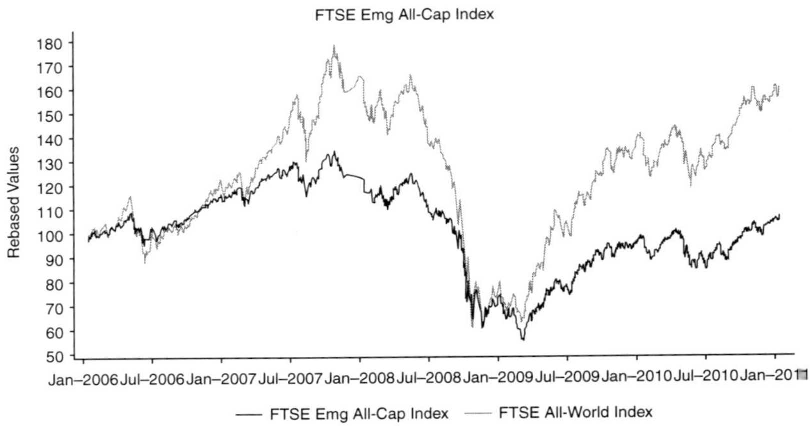

Figure 2.1 Comparison of the performance of the FTSE Emerging Markets Index and the FTSE All World Index from 2006
Source: FTSE, 2011.

In addition to the FTSEs, there are other lists from specialised institutions like ISI Emerging Markets or indexes like the Morgan Stanley Capital International (MSCI). In fact, Jim O'Neill from Goldman Sachs, the creator of BRIC, recently proposed to add Mexico, South Korea, Turkey and Indonesia to what he dubs 'growth markets' as 'any economy from the emerging markets world that is already 1% of global GDP or more, and has the potential for that to rise, has the ability to be taken seriously'.[6]

But still it seems challenging to create a comprehensive list, index or even a definition of emerging economies. One of the reasons is that countries are growing; markets may have developed from a past emerging market phase like South Korea or Taiwan (or the other way around, like Argentina). A second reason may be the simplification inherent in making an index; for example, small countries (or countries with limited market liquidity), like Chile, are often underestimated.

2.3 Trade and investments

In any case, and regardless of different classifications, the increasing importance of LEDCs or emerging markets is being fed by their growing share in the flows of trade and investments in the world economy. This can be seen in Figure 2.2: by 1970 merchandise exports were around

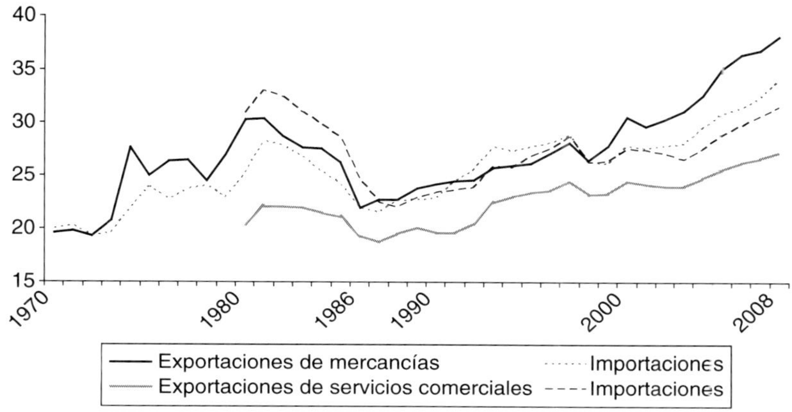

Figure 2.2 Share of developing economies in world trade in per cent, 1970–2008

Source: WTO, 2010a.

20% and by 2008 they had reached 38%; commercial services exports also increased from around 20% in 1970 to 27% of global trade in 2008 (WTO, 2010a).

A comparison between Table 2.2 and Table 2.3 shows the same trend by country and region. In, Table 2.2 it is possible to see that the EU 15, the United States and Japan accounted for around 65% and 60% of world trade in 1990 and 1999 respectively, and that LEDCs accounted for only around 12% and 18% over the same period. Ten years later, Table 2.3 shows that in 2009 the EU 27, the United States and Japan accounted for around 33.5% while the Six East Asian Traders,[7] China, Mexico and the Russian Federation were responsible for 34% of world trade. From Table 2.3, it is also worth noting that the list of top ten exporters is shared by developed countries and emerging markets, and also that India and Brazil (key components in the BRIC) are still at an early stage in their involvement in international trade with 1.7% (position 15) and 1.6% (position 18) respectively.

For foreign investments the trend is similar. As can be seen in Figure 2.3, FDI flows to developing and transition economies have been growing, from a 10% share in 1974 to 49% of total flows in 2009. If this trend continues, in a few years emerging markets for the first time will be receiving more FDI than developed economies. This trend is also seen in mergers and acquisitions (M&A). Year 2010 figures in emerging

Table 2.2 World merchandise exports by country and region in %, 1999

	Share		Annual percentage change			
	1990	1999	1990–99	1997	1998	1999
Developed countries						
European Union (15)	44.5	39.8	4	0	4	–1
United States	11.6	12.7	7	10	–1	2
Japan	8.5	7.7	4	2	–8	8
	64.6	**60.2**				
LEDCs						
Six East Asian traders	7.9	10.0	8	3	–7	8
China	1.8	3.6	14	21	0	6
Mexico	1.2	2.5	14	15	6	16
Central and Eastern Europe	1.4	1.9	7	6	9	1
	12.3	**17.9**				
Regions						
Western Europe	48.3	43.0	4	–1	4	0
Asia	21.8	25.5	7	5	–6	8
North America	15.4	17.1	7	9	–1	4
Latin America	4.3	5.4	8	11	–1	6
C./E. Europe/Baltic States/CIS	3.1	3.9	6	4	–5	–1
Middle East	4.0	3.1	3	5	–23	24
Africa	3.1	2.0	1	2	–16	9
Regional Trade Associations						
NAFTA (3)	16.6	19.6	7	10	0	6
MERCOSUR (4)	1.4	1.4	5	11	–2	–9
ASEAN (10)	4.3	6.6	11	4	–7	9

Source: WTO, 2000.

markets are now higher than those of Europe for the first time with a volume of US $575.7 billion against Europe's $550.2 billion. 'Deals by companies in emerging markets now account for 30% of global M&A activity, while Europe's share has fallen to 29%. China, with about $133 billion in deals, has attracted most interest this year from acquirers. Brazil, India and Russia follow, with the four BRIC countries together accounting for more than half of emerging markets activity' (Saigol and Thomas, 2010).

Table 2.3 World merchandise exports and imports by country in %, 2009

Rank	Exporters	Share	Rank	Importers	Share
1	Extra-EU (27) exports	16.2	1	Extra-EU (27) imports	17.4
2	China	12.7	2	United States	16.7
3	United States	11.2	3	China	10.5
4	Japan	6.2	4	Japan	5.7
5	Korea, Republic of	3.9	5	Hong Kong, China	3.7
6	Hong Kong, China	3.5	6	Canada[a]	3.4
7	Canada	3.4	7	Korea, Republic of	3.4
8	Russian Federation	3.2	8	India	2.6
9	Singapore	2.9	9	Singapore	2.6
10	Mexico	2.4	10	Mexico	2.5
	Sub Total	**65.5**		**Sub Total**	**65.9**
11	Taipei, Chinese	2.2	11	Russian Federation	2.0
12	Saudi Arabia	2.0	12	Taipei, Chinese	1.8
13	United Arab Emirates[b]	1.9	13	Australia	1.7
14	Switzerland	1.8	14	Switzerland	1.6
15	India	1.7	15	Turkey	1.5
16	Malaysia	1.7	16	United Arab Emirates[b]	1.5
17	Australia	1.6	17	Thailand	1.4
18	Brazil	1.6	18	Brazil	1.4
19	Thailand	1.6	19	Malaysia	1.3
20	Norway	1.3	20	Saudi Arabia	1.0
21	Indonesia	1.3	21	Indonesia	1.0
22	Turkey	1.1	22	South Africa	0.8
23	Iran, Islamic Rep. of	0.8	23	Viet Nam	0.7
24	South Africa	0.7	24	Norway	0.7
25	Bolivarian Rep. of Venezuela	0.6	25	Iran, Islamic Rep. of	0.5
26	Viet Nam	0.6	26	Israel	0.5
27	Argentina	0.6	27	Philippines	0.5
28	Chile	0.6	28	Ukraine	0.5
29	Nigeria[b]	0.6	29	Egypt	0.5
30	Kuwait	0.5	30	Chile	0.4
31	Israel	0.5	31	Bolivarian Rep. of Venezuela	0.4
32	Algeria	0.5	32	Algeria	0.4
33	Kazakhstan	0.5	33	Nigeria[b]	0.4
34	Qatar[b]	0.4	34	Argentina	0.4
35	Angola	0.4	35	Iraq[b]	0.4

Notes: [a] Imports are valued f.o.b.
[b] Secretariat estimates.
Source: WTO, 2010b.

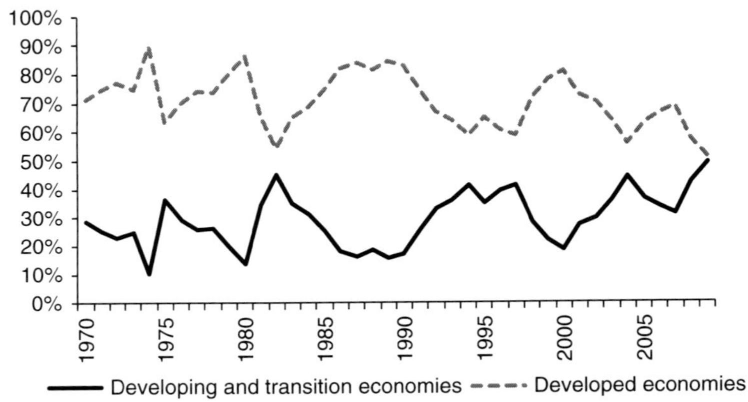

Figure 2.3 Inward and outward FDI flows, annual, 1970–2009
Source: UNCTAD, 2011.

In any case, not all emerging economies are active recipients of FDI. Fifteen countries from East Asia, Latin America and Southern Africa account for around 73% of inward FDI to developing economies as can be seen in Table 2.4. Recipients in this table are ranked by the stock of FDI, where it is worth noting the high position of a small country like Chile (probably the gateway for foreign investments in South America) showing that not only big countries can be emerging economies. India's relatively low position is also worth mention as its FDI stocks are much lower than its BRIC counterparts.

2.4 Main characteristics

As stated above, it is difficult to find a comprehensive definition of emerging markets that suits all. For example, 'for households, emerging markets are the source of cheap consumer goods. For frustrated computer users, they are often the location of outsourced technical support. For executives of multinationals, emerging markets are growth drivers amid stagnation and financial crisis in developed economies' (Khanna and Palepu, 2010, p. 1).

But one of the criteria that often underlies various definitions of emerging markets 'is the system of market governance and, in particular, the extent and stability of a free market system' (Arnold and Quelch, 1998, p. 8) along with the 'ease with which transactions can take place in any market and the cost associated with it' (Khanna and Palepu, 2002, p. 4).

Table 2.4 FDI inward stock to developing economies, 1990–2009, in millions of US dollars

Developing economies[a]		**26,836,498**	**(%)**
1	China	3,793,786	14.14
2	Brazil	2,652,972	9.89
3	Mexico	2,588,323	9.64
4	Russian Federation	1,840,589	6.86
5	Chile	981,911	3.66
6	Korea, Republic of	974,455	3.63
7	Argentina	923,725	3.44
8	South Africa	851,992	3.17
9	Malaysia	815,441	3.04
10	Thailand	795,430	2.96
11	Turkey	743,011	2.77
12	British Virgin Islands	724,764	2.70
13	India	704,872	2.63
14	Saudi Arabia	699,253	2.61
15	Indonesia	591,238	2.20
		Total	**73.34**
East Asia[b]		5,439,300	20.27
South and Central America[c]		9,107,029	33.94
Southern Africa[d]		1,238,610	4.62
		Total	**58.82**

Notes: [a] Hong Kong and Singapore were withdrawn by the authors from UNCTAD's list of developing economies following Hoskisson et al.'s (2000) list of emerging countries; the total FDI stock in developing economies shown in the table does not include the stock in these countries.

[b] China; Korea, Democratic People's Republic of; Korea, Republic of; Macao, China; Mongolia; Taiwan Province of China.

[c] Argentina; Plurinational State of Bolivia; Brazil; Chile; Colombia; Ecuador; Guyana; Paraguay; Peru; Suriname; Uruguay; Bolivarian Republic of Venezuela; Belize; Costa Rica; El Salvador; Guatemala; Honduras; Mexico; Nicaragua; Panama.

[d] Angola; Botswana; Lesotho; Malawi; Mozambique; Namibia; South Africa; Swaziland; Zambia; Zimbabwe.

Source: UNCTAD, 2010.

This is based on the fact that economies should put in place a web of institutions to facilitate the efficient functioning of markets. These institutions mould the social and organisational behaviour of organisations and, as a consequence, affect their decision-making processes as well as their available options. Institutions in a market (country) should reduce uncertainty and provide a stable, level playing field that facilitates interactions and diminishes both transaction and information costs.

This complex web of institutions that permeates the developed economies is either absent or poorly developed in emerging markets. This seems evident in three main areas in EMs: (1) information problems: comprehensive, reliable and objective information to make decisions is not widely available; (2) misguided regulations: some emerging economies place political goals over economic efficiency, which reduces the chances to take full advantage of business opportunities; and (3) inefficient judicial systems; an independent judicial system that enforces contracts in a reliable and predictable way does not seem to be the reality in EMs (Khanna and Palepu, 1997).

In this sense, it has been found that 'building all the institutional infrastructure for well-functioning markets is a slow and time consuming process' (Khanna and Palepu, 2002, p. 4). Reasons for this can be: (1) that emerging markets require good political governance to develop institutions with thoughtful and supportive regulations, as well as even-handed and predictable enforcement; (2) that these institutions need qualified persons with certain skills who are usually difficult to find in emerging economies; and (3) that in the development of market institutions there is a mutual interdependence across the first two problems (Hoskisson et al., 2000; Khanna and Palepu, 2002). In fact, it has been suggested that 'many emerging markets are likely to suffer from significant institutional voids for a long time to come' (Khanna and Palepu, 2002, p. 4) as 'the mere deregulation of economies does not automatically lead to immediate reduction in transaction costs' (Khanna and Palepu, 2000, p. 281).

Institutional voids usually result in higher transaction costs. This is because the price system does not give reliable information for the efficient allocation of resources; also, because sometimes the government's discretion rather than the rule of law determines property rights and makes their enforcement more costly.

Institutional voids can also lead to market failures and, as a consequence, firms operating in EMs often have to perform some of these functions themselves. Higher transaction costs are also behind the high prevalence in emerging markets of unrelated diversified local business groups, mainly due to the low development of the capital and labour markets. Examples of this are the chaebols in South Korea, business houses of India, or grupos económicos in Latin America (Khanna and Palepu, 1997).

In addition, capabilities for relationship-based management in emerging markets substitute for the lack of institutional infrastructure as firms tend to base their competitive advantage on links with local authorities. In this environment, local companies can obtain licences and other benefits due to their close links with the home government and, as a consequence, protect their operations from domestic and international competitors (Fornes, 2009; Hoskisson et al., 2000).

2.5 Local players

Local companies from emerging countries usually take any of these three organisational forms: (1) domestic competitors (mainly business groups, state-owned companies, and privatised firms); (2) entrepreneurial start-ups; and (3) overseas players (Peng, 2003; Peng, Tan and Tong, 2004). They face four broad challenges: (1) competition from developed countries' firms entering EMs to exploit the skills developed in their home markets; (2) having to develop new strategies to deal with improved conditions in their domestic markets; (3) having to enter other EMs to exploit the strengths developed in their domestic markets; and (4) having to enter developed economies (Wright, Filatotchev, Hoskisson, and Peng, 2005).

These companies face a 'high velocity' environment of rapid political, economic and institutional changes' (Wright et al., 2005, p. 7). Due to this, EMs' companies have developed a set of abilities, strengths and capabilities (like close links with governments, structures aimed at internalising transaction costs, etc.) to overcome these challenges which help them to compete successfully in the domestic market. But their engagement in international activities, especially FDI, has been relatively low.

In the 1990s, most FDI from EMs was categorised as asset-exploitation and asset-seeking. The former implies a transfer of proprietary assets across the border, and the latter aims at the acquisition of strategic assets (Makino, Chung-Ming, and Rhy-Song, 2002).

Asset-exploitation FDI by EMs' firms, especially in other developing countries, is usually small scale, labour intensive and has flexible production skills along with products suitable for the host market that could eventually replace domestic competition. Companies from EMs used to choose FDI, rather than exports or licensing, as their preferred option because of: (1) the uncertainty of the local market (mainly poor information on the value of local assets and weak distribution networks), (2) the difficulty for local firms to internationalise their operations and (3) the weak legal framework to protect technological knowledge (Wells, 1981, 1983).

Asset-seeking FDI has been followed mainly by companies from Asia's newly industrialised economies to reinforce their price competitiveness in EMs, but to strengthen their non-price competitiveness when investing in developed countries (Chen and Chen, 1998; Kumar, 1998). This strategy implies that internal strengths should come from the ownership of proprietary assets and also from the capacity to buy and the knowledge to manage assets from firms in the host country (Dunning, 1995; Dunning, 1998).

But since the 2000s, the situation has been changing as firms from EMs have been increasing their presence outside their home markets. Well known examples like Cemex and America Móvil from Mexico, Ternium from Argentina, Vale and Gerdau from Brazil, JSFC from Russia, Lenovo and ZTE from China and Tata Motors from India are leading the way in the internationalisation of companies from emerging economies followed by an increasing number of firms engaging in international operations. This trend can be seen in Table 2.5, which shows the outward stock of FDI as a percentage of GDP. In the table, it is worth noting the high increases during the period of countries like Chile, Malaysia, Korea or South Africa, although they are still far away from the 40.8% posted by developed economies.

Different from the situation for most of the twentieth century, EMs' companies now seem to be in a stronger position to compete in foreign markets. These companies can offer high levels of flexibility and the capability for rapid adjustment from their experience dealing with changing home environments. They can also offer everyday low prices and high value for the money to middle and low segments of consumers in both developed and emerging economies. Firms from EMs have also been strengthening their position as suppliers of global retailers where customers are now demanding their products (Williamson and Yin, 2009).

Still, they seem to have a long way to go until they can reach a level of internationalisation (measured by foreign assets) similar to that of their Western counterparts. This is self-evident in a comparison between the figures in Table 2.6 (the top 75 nonfinancial firms from EMs) with the world's top 75 MNEs (UNCTAD, 2010). For example, General Electric, the world leader, has US $401.290 million in foreign assets, while CITIC from China (topping the EMs' list) has around 10% of this value (CITIC is number 48 in the world's list). Also, the no. 75 company in the world's top 100 MNEs, TeliaSonera AB from Sweden, has US $29.067 million in foreign assets, while TPV Technology Limited from China has less than 10% of this figure in foreign assets (US $2,266 million).

Table 2.5 FDI outward stock as percentage of GDP, 1990–2009

	1990	1991	1992	1993	1994	1995	1996	1997	1998	1999	2000	2001	2002	2003	2004	2005	2006	2007	2008	2009
China	1.1	1.3	1.9	2.1	2.7	2.3	2.2	2.3	2.4	2.4	2.3	2.6	2.6	2.0	2.3	2.6	2.8	2.8	3.4	4.9
Brazil	9.4	10.3	10.8	9.7	7.9	5.8	5.2	5.2	5.7	8.5	8.1	9.0	10.8	9.9	10.4	9.0	10.5	10.0	9.9	10.0
Mexico	1.0	0.9	1.0	0.8	1.1	1.5	1.3	1.3	1.4	1.6	1.4	1.9	2.0	2.6	3.2	3.3	3.7	4.1	4.2	6.1
Russian Federation	..	..	..	0.5	0.6	0.8	1.1	1.9	3.3	4.9	7.8	14.4	18.1	21.0	18.1	19.2	22.0	28.8	12.1	20.1
Chile	0.5	0.7	1.5	2.3	3.6	3.8	5.2	6.2	8.5	12.3	14.8	17.1	18.2	18.5	18.2	18.1	17.7	19.3	18.6	25.2
Korea, Republic of	0.9	1.1	1.3	1.5	1.8	2.0	2.5	3.3	5.9	5.2	5.0	4.0	3.6	3.9	4.5	4.6	5.2	7.1	10.5	13.9
Argentina	4.3	3.2	3.2	3.4	3.6	4.1	4.5	5.5	6.1	7.1	7.4	7.9	20.2	16.6	14.2	12.7	12.1	10.5	8.7	9.5
South Africa	13.4	13.4	13.6	13.8	14.1	15.4	16.9	15.6	20.0	24.8	24.3	14.8	19.8	16.2	17.8	15.3	19.5	23.0	18.0	22.6
Malaysia	1.7	1.6	1.8	2.1	3.5	5.8	8.8	11.5	17.2	17.5	16.9	9.0	10.1	10.9	10.3	15.9	23.1	31.3	30.5	39.5
Thailand	0.5	0.6	0.7	0.8	1.0	1.4	1.7	1.3	2.4	2.5	1.8	2.3	2.3	2.4	2.3	2.9	3.1	4.0	4.6	6.2
Turkey	0.6	0.6	0.6	0.5	0.8	0.6	0.6	0.7	0.8	1.1	1.4	2.3	2.5	2.0	1.8	1.7	1.7	1.9	1.9	2.4
India	0.0	0.0	0.1	0.1	0.1	0.1	0.2	0.1	0.2	0.4	0.4	0.5	0.8	1.0	1.1	1.2	2.9	3.7	4.9	6.1
Saudi Arabia	1.8	1.5	1.6	1.7	1.8	1.8	1.8	1.9	2.3	2.1	2.6	2.8	3.7	3.5	3.0	4.5	5.5	8.4	7.2	11.1
Indonesia	0.1	0.1	0.5	0.7	2.4	2.7	2.6	2.8	6.4	4.4	4.2	4.3	3.7	3.2	4.2	4.9	4.6	4.9	5.3	5.6
Japan	6.7	6.7	6.6	6.0	5.8	4.5	5.6	6.4	7.0	5.7	6.0	7.3	7.8	7.9	8.0	8.5	10.3	12.4	13.9	14.6
Canada	14.6	15.8	15.2	16.4	18.5	20.0	21.6	24.0	27.9	30.5	32.8	35.0	37.5	36.8	37.6	34.3	34.8	36.5	35.0	42.4
United States	12.6	13.8	12.6	16.0	15.8	18.6	20.7	22.8	26.2	30.8	27.6	23.0	19.4	25.0	28.9	29.4	34.0	38.3	21.8	30.2
United Kingdom	23.1	22.4	20.6	25.5	26.6	26.8	27.7	27.2	34.3	46.8	62.3	60.6	63.2	63.8	56.6	52.6	59.6	65.6	57.5	76.0
Italy	5.3	5.9	5.6	7.9	8.5	9.4	9.3	11.7	14.5	15.1	16.4	16.3	16.0	15.9	16.2	16.5	20.3	24.6	22.3	27.4
Spain	3.0	3.7	4.5	5.9	5.6	5.8	7.2	9.3	12.3	19.1	22.2	23.6	23.8	25.0	27.0	27.0	35.3	40.8	37.4	44.2
France	9.0	10.6	11.4	12.3	13.4	13.0	14.7	16.7	19.6	22.9	69.7	59.6	43.8	52.6	56.1	57.5	71.0	69.6	45.9	64.9
Germany	8.8	9.6	8.6	9.3	10.5	10.6	11.9	14.3	17.1	19.3	28.5	32.7	34.5	34.0	33.7	33.2	37.1	40.1	36.0	41.2
Developed economies	11.2	11.9	11.2	12.9	13.3	14.0	15.8	18.0	21.5	24.7	28.8	27.8	26.8	30.7	32.6	32.7	38.9	42.8	32.9	40.8

Source: UNCTAD, 2010.

Table 2.6 The top 75 nonfinancial firms from developing and transition economies, ranked by foreign assets, 2008[a]

				Assets		Sales			
	Corporation	Home economy	Industry[b]	Foreign	%	Total	Foreign	Total	TNI %[c]
1	CITIC Group	China	Diversified	43,750	18	238,725	5,427	22,230	21.0
2	Cemex S.A.	Mexico	Nonmetallic mineral products	40,258	89	45,084	17,982	21,830	81.6
3	Samsung Electronics Co., Ltd.	Korea, Republic of	Electrical and electronic equipment	28,765	34	83,738	88,892	110,321	54.2
4	Petronas – Petroliam Nasional Bhd	Malaysia	Petroleum expl./ref./distr.	28,447	27	106,416	32,477	77,094	29.6
5	Hyundai Motor Company	Korea, Republic of	Motor vehicles	28,359	35	82,072	33,874	72,523	36.5
6	China Ocean Shipping (Group) Company	China	Transport and storage	28,066	77	36,253	18,041	27,431	49.9
7	Lukoil	Russian Federation	Petroleum and natural gas	21,515	30	71,461	87,637	107,680	42.2
8	Vale S.A	Brazil	Mining and quarrying	19,635	25	79,931	30,939	37,426	38.3
9	Petróleos De Venezuela	Venezuela, Bolivarian Republic of	Petroleum expl./ref./distr.	19,244	15	131,832	52,494	126,364	21.5
10	Zain	Kuwait	Telecommunications	18,746	95	19,761	6,034	7,452	61.2
11	Formosa Plastics Group	Taiwan Province of China	Chemicals	16,937	22	76,587	17,078	66,259	40.9
12	Tata Steel Ltd.	India	Metal and metal products	16,826	70	23,868	26,426	32,168	69.8

13	Petroleo Brasileiro S.A. – Petrobras	Brazil	Petroleum expl./ref./distr.	15,075	12	125,695	40,179	146,529	16.2
14	Hon Hai Precision Industries	Taiwan Province of China	Electrical & electronic equipment	14,664	55	26,771	21,727	61,810	58.1
15	Metalurgica Gerdau S.A.	Brazil	Metal and metal products	13,658	53	25,750	10,274	23,182	48.6
16	Abu Dhabi National Energy Company	United Arab Emirates	Utilities (Electricity, gas and water)	13,519	57	23,523	3,376	4,576	69.5
17	Oil And Natural Gas Corporation	India	Petroleum expl./ref./distr.	13,477	44	30,456	4,238	27,684	23.8
18	MTN Group Limited	South Africa	Telecommunications	13,266	73	18,281	7,868	12,403	67.4
19	LG Corp.	Korea, Republic of	Electrical and electronic equipment	13,256	26	51,517	44,439	82,060	43.8
20	Evraz	Russian Federation	Metal and metal products	11,196	58	19,448	12,805	20,380	47.5
21	Qatar Telecom	Qatar	Telecommunications	10,598	52	20,412	4,077	5,582	69.7
22	América Móvil	Mexico	Telecommunications	10,428	33	31,481	17,323	31,026	52.6
23	China National Petroleum Corporation	China	Petroleum expl./ref./distr.	9,409	4	264,016	4,384	165,224	2.7
24	Hindalco Industries Limited	India	Diversified	8,564	68	12,653	11,371	14,338	71.6
25	STX Corporation	Korea, Republic of	Other equipments goods	8,308	45	18,338	1,668	12,914	34.5

Continued

Table 2.6 Continued

	Corporation	Home economy	Industry [b]	Assets		Sales			
				Foreign	%	Total	Foreign	Total	TNI % [c]
26	Axiata Group Bhd	Malaysia	Telecommunications	8,184	76	10,783	1,746	3,406	67.7
27	Severstal	Russian Federation	Metal and metal products	8,066	36	22,480	9,325	22,393	30.2
28	Ternium SA	Argentina	Metal and metal products	7,063	66	10,671	5,357	8,465	64.5
29	China State Construction Engineering Corp	China	Construction and real estate	7,015	23	29,873	3,619	29,080	16.6
30	YTL Corp. Berhad	Malaysia	Utilities (Electricity, gas and water)	7,014	63	11,102	968	1,966	47.8
31	Tata Motors Ltd.	India	Automobile	6,767	47	14,359	9,869	15,635	48.9
32	Asustek Computer Inc	Taiwan Province of China	Electrical and electronic equipment	6,746	61	10,998	9,522	21,157	55.9
33	Orascom Telecom Holding	Egypt	Telecommunications	6,718	69	9,757	2,947	5,305	64.4
34	Quanta Computer Inc	Taiwan Province of China	Electrical and electronic equipment	6,711	73	9,250	4,930	25,946	41.6
35	Sasol Limited	South Africa	Chemicals	6,679	35	18,977	7,781	21,676	29.6
36	Sinochem Corp.	China	Petroleum expl./ref./distr.	6,409	32	19,825	34,218	44,280	36.8
37	Sappi Limited	South Africa	Wood and paper products	5,933	97	6,109	5,483	5,863	85.2
38	JSFC Sistema	Russian Federation	Telecommunications	5,698	20	29,159	3,983	16,671	19.1
39	Netcare Limited	South Africa	Other consumer services	5,590	84	6,642	1,516	2,904	56.1
40	Posco	Korea, Republic of	Metal and metal products	5,335	14	37,345	13,512	37,966	21.4
41	Suzlon Energy Limited	India	Diversified	5,310	72	7,370	4,714	5,685	75.7

42	China National Offshore Oil Corp.	China	Petroleum expl./ref./distr.	5,247	9	59,917	4,475	28,028	9.4
43	Genting Berhad	Malaysia	Other consumer services	5,139	58	8,790	667	2,726	47.9
44	Steinhoff International holdings	South Africa	Other consumer goods	5,060	70	7,194	3,492	5,636	56.5
45	Gold Fields Limited	South Africa	Metal and metal products	4,839	57	8,491	1,443	3,223	35.7
46	Medi Clinic Corp. Limited	South Africa	Other consumer services	4,788	89	5,395	1,341	2,294	78.7
47	Pou Chen Corp.	Taiwan Province of China	Other consumer goods	4,553	66	6,929	5,518	6,622	71.6
48	Acer Inc.	Taiwan Province of China	Electrical and electronic equipment	4,455	60	7,418	16,495	17,311	79.9
49	MMC Norilsk Nickel	Russian Federation		4,389	21	20,823	1,998	13,980	13.3
50	Sime Darby Berhad	Malaysia	Diversified	4,307	43	10,061	6,065	8,827	45.7
51	China Communications Construction Co.	China	Construction and real estate	4,010	13	31,911	5,599	25,740	12.1
52	Telefonos De Mexico S.A. De C.V.	Mexico	Telecommunications	3,948	29	13,528	2,464	11,140	28.6
53	Naspers Limited	South Africa	Other consumer services	3,821	66	5,746	995	3,018	55.3
54	Taiwan Semiconductor Manufacturing Co Ltd.	Taiwan Province of China	Electrical and electronic equipment	3,813	22	17,030	6,139	10,558	30.8

Continued

Table 2.6 Continued

	Corporation	Home economy	Industry[b]	Assets			Sales		
				Foreign	%	Total	Foreign	Total	TNI %[c]
55	VimpelCom	Russian Federation	Telecommunications	3,726	24	15,725	1,520	10,117	21.8
56	Beijing Enterprises Holdings Ltd.	China	Diversified	3,662	55	6,670	2,524	2,530	77.0
57	Enka Insaat ve Sanayi	Turkey	Construction and real estate	3,540	46	7,767	3,256	6,956	46.5
58	FEMSA-Fomento Economico Mexicano	Mexico	Food, beverages and tobacco	3,508	26	13,377	4,792	15,082	30.3
59	China Railway Construction Corporation Ltd.	China	Construction	3,146	10	32,204	2,475	31,571	9.1
60	ZTE Corp.	China	Other consumer goods	3,143	41	7,642	3,860	6,373	44.2
61	Chi MEI Optoelectronics	Taiwan Province of China	Electrical and electronic equipment	3,070	17	18,099	187	10,081	11.9
62	Mechel	Russian Federation	Metal and metal products	2,911	24	12,010	1,385	9,951	16.0
63	United Microelectronics Corporation	Taiwan Province of China	Electrical and electronic equipment	2,901	44	6,594	2,153	3,068	52.7
64	Inventec Company	Taiwan Province of China	Electrical and electronic equipment	2,874	73	3,935	1,911	12,016	61.2
65	Lenovo Group	China	Electrical and electronic equipment	2,732	43	6,308	8,467	14,901	41.1
66	San Miguel Corporation	Philippines	Food, beverages and tobacco	2,655	37	7,117	458	3,774	21.7

67	Compal Electronics Inc	Taiwan Province of China	Other consumer goods	2,573	43	5,954	4,579	15,171	43.9
68	PTT Public Company Limited	Thailand	Petroleum expl./ref./distr.	2,525	10	25,252	5,993	59,931	10.0
69	National Industries Group Holdings SAK	Kuwait	Diversified	2,504	40	6,279	264	420	47.5
70	Tanjong Public Limited Company	Malaysia	Pharmaceuticals	2,445	71	3,451	455	1,101	49.5
71	Qisda Corp. (Benq)	Taiwan Province of China	Electrical and electronic equipment	2,441	62	3,936	2,678	5,372	53.5
72	TMK	Russian Federation	Metal and metal products	2,361	33	7,071	2,302	5,690	27.4
73	Wistron Corp.	Taiwan Province of China	Other equipments goods	2,316	55	4,249	2,458	14,153	42.7
74	China Minmetals Corp.	China	Metal and metal products	2,269	17	13,484	4,318	26,668	11.6
75	TPV Technology Limited	China	Wholesale trade	2,266	68	3,354	6,860	9,247	69.8

Notes: [a] Hong Kong and Singapore were withdrawn by the authors from UNCTAD's list of developing economies following Hoskisson et al.'s (2000) list of emerging countries.
[b] Industry classification for companies follows the United States Standard Industrial Classification as used by the United States Securities and Exchange Commission (SEC).
[c] TNI, the Transnationlity Index, is calculated as the average of the following three ratios: foreign assets to total assets, foreign sales to total sales and foreign employment to total employment.
Source: UNCTAD, 2010.

2.6 Emerging cities

Probably due to the heritage from the time when the idea of less economically developed countries was in use, EMs have continued to be associated with countries rather than with markets. This difference is relevant as one of the characteristics of these countries is the disparity in income distribution, in which most of the wealth is concentrated in their cities and surrounding areas, usually large ones. This is the case for small countries, like Chile, where its capital, Santiago, has a population of around 5 million (out of the country's total population of 16 million), or bigger countries, like Argentina, where Buenos Aires, the capital city, has around 18 million inhabitants (including La Plata) out of the country's total population of around 40 million. Brazil has two cities, Sao Paulo and Rio de Janeiro, with around 20 million and 12 million people respectively, out of an estimated population for the country of 196 million. In Mexico City, there are more than 20 million inhabitants out of the country's total population of around 112 million. Similar cases can be found in China, where the five largest and most developed cities of Shanghai, Nanjing, Guangzhou, Hangzhou, and Beijing account for a population of around 75 million. Examples like these can be found in most emerging markets. As a comparison, in the EU there are only two urban areas with populations of around 10 million (London and Paris); the same is true in the United States (New York and Los Angeles) and in Japan (Tokyo and Osaka).

These cities are the real emerging markets. They are the places where a growing middle class is demanding higher living standards as the economy develops and where growth rates are usually higher than those in developed economies. Most of these cities have vibrant economies with an average purchasing power higher than the rest of the country and they are the places where the local wealthy live. Although these cities suffer from some of the institutional voids present in their countries, private agencies operate in these markets to help in the reduction of inefficiencies in transactions (to the extent permitted by local legislation), physical infrastructure is improving along with public transportation and educational levels and reach are also improving. Table 2.7 shows projections of the 30 largest urban agglomerations in 2025, where it can be seen that the great majority of cities are in emerging economies (24 out of 30). These 24 cities will total 375 million inhabitants in 2025, 75% of the current population of the 27 countries in the EU (Eurostat, 201).

Table 2.7 Projections of the 30 largest urban agglomerations in 2025 ranked by population size

	Urban agglomeration	Country	Estimated population
1	Tokyo	Japan	37.09
2	Delhi	India	28.57
3	Mumbai (Bombay)	India	25.81
4	São Paulo	Brazil	21.65
5	Dhaka	Bangladesh	20.94
6	Ciudad de México (Mexico City)	Mexico	20.71
7	New York–Newark	United States of America	20.64
8	Kolkata (Calcutta)	India	20.11
9	Shanghai	China	20.02
10	Karachi	Pakistan	18.73
11	Lagos	Nigeria	15.81
12	Kinshasa	Democratic Republic of the Congo	15.04
13	Beijing	China	15.02
14	Manila	Philippines	14.92
15	Buenos Aires	Argentina	13.71
16	Los Angeles–Long Beach-Santa Ana	United States of America	13.68
17	Al-Qahirah (Cairo)	Egypt	13.53
18	Rio de Janeiro	Brazil	12.65
19	Istanbul	Turkey	12.11
20	Osaka-Kobe	Japan	11.37
21	Shenzhen	China	11.15
22	Chongqing	China	11.07
23	Guangzhou	China	10.96
24	Paris	France	10.88
25	Jakarta	Indonesia	10.85
26	Moskva (Moscow)	Russian Federation	10.66
27	Bogotá	Colombia	10.54
28	Lima	Peru	10.53
29	Lahore	Pakistan	10.31
30	Chicago	United States of America	9.94

Source: UN, 2009b.

2.7 China–Latin America: the emerging markets' axis

It is widely agreed that most of the current status attained by EMs started with the Six East Asian Traders in the 1970s and 1980s and it has been consolidated with the emergence of China from the 2000s. But there are other emerging markets that have been increasing their presence in the world's economy since the 1990s, such as Chile and Mexico, and from the 2000s, Brazil and Costa Rica. In fact, most Latin American countries in the last decade have been posting growth rates much higher than those in developed economies led mainly by an export boom. Asia is increasingly the destination of these exports, whereas China has become a main trading partner for many Latin American countries. At the same time, Latin America, with around 600 million people and a common culture, history and language,[8] has also been a target market for many Chinese companies looking for consumers for their low-cost products.

The trade relationship between China and Latin America was negligible at the beginning of the 1990s. But from the mid-1990s it has grown around 20 times (posting a trade surplus for China of around US $47 billion in 2008 from a deficit of US $283 million in 1990 [ECLAC, 2010c; Sanchez Ancochea, 2006]). A similar situation can be described for investments. One of the main destinations of Chinese Outward Foreign Direct Investment (ODI) in recent years has been Latin America, with 50% of Chinese ODI in 2004 (more than the 30% that went towards Asia) (Blazquez-Lidoy, Rodriguez, and Santiso, 2006, p. 35), with 53% in 2005, 40% in 2006 (MOFCOM, 2007) and with similar trends in 2008 and 2009 (MOFCOM, 2008).

This shows that a new strong axis of trade and investments between China and LA is consolidating. Flows of trade and investment exceed US $100 billion (ECLAC, 2008, 2010c) and are growing at an annual rate close to 50% (WTO, 2008). This figure is similar to that of the trade between the EU and Japan at the end of the 1990s, which means that the China–LA axis rivals that of the Triad's[9] axes (Fornes and Butt-Philip, 2011b). In other words, the last decade has seen the development of the China–Latin America commercial relationship as the emerging markets' axis (Fornes, 2011).

2.8 Conclusion

This chapter has introduced the growing economic relationship between China and Latin America, the focus of this book, by placing it within the wider context of emerging markets and their increasing presence in the world's economy. The next chapter will analyse in detail this relationship, and will also study its main actors.

3
China–Latin America: The Emerging Markets' Axis

> The expanding link between Asia and Latin America is symbolic of the economic shakeout going on worldwide ... with Europe, Japan and the US retreating from their roles as omnipotent centres to leave space for a more balanced configuration.
>
> Javier Santiso, former chief development economist and director of the OECD Development Centre.[1]

3.1 Introduction

A new strong axis of trade and investments between China and Latin America is developing. Flows of trade and investment are exceeding US $100 billion (ECLAC, 2008, 2010c), a figure similar to the trade from the EU to Japan at the end of 1990s.

This new axis appears to be different from economic relations between China and other emerging markets as trade is growing in the two directions (not one, towards China, as it is mainly the case, for example, with African countries); in fact, imports from China to Latin America are growing faster than exports! Trade between China and Latin America has increased more than 25 times since 1995 due mainly to the Chinese demand for raw materials (such as soya, iron ore, copper, etc.), because Latin America appears as one of the most complementary trade partners for China, and also because Chinese manufacturers are finding an increasing demand in Latin American markets for their low and intermediate technology products (ECLAC, 2006; Fornes and Butt-Philip, 2009, 2011b; Lapper, 2007; Santiso, 2006a).

The trade flows are the result of, among other things, investment and trade agreements signed between China and Argentina, Brazil, Chile and Peru in 2004, with Venezuela in 2006, a Free Trade Agreement (FTA) between Chile and China signed in 2005 (Bravo, 2006) (see Appendix 3), a FTA signed between Peru and China (La Tercera, 2007b; MOFCOM, 2009c) (see Appendix 5), a FTA signed between Costa Rica and China in 2010 (see Appendix 6), and China's membership of the Inter-American Development Bank (Lapper, 2007). In addition, China has committed investments of around US $100 billion in the region before 2015 (La Nación, 2004d; Painter, 2008; Sanchez Ancochea, 2006).

3.2 China–Latin America

'As early as 1761, the French sinologist De Giognes proposed that the New World was discovered not by Columbus, but by the Chinese. Lengthy debates resulted in no consensus on this historical issue, and it finally quieted down in the West. But then some Chinese scholars started to take interest in this hypothesis, and used classical Chinese writings and even some archaeological findings to support their argument that, as early as the fifth century, a Chinese monk (or master) named Hui Sen arrived in what is now called Mexico, then known as Fu-sang in Chinese. Needless to say, many more Chinese historians said that this was complete nonsense' (Shixue, 2007, p. 2).

More recently, from 1978 and based on the reforms by Deng Xiaoping, China changed its foreign policy towards Latin America and the Caribbean. As a consequence, 'China abandoned its political strategy of expanding Maoism to Latin America' and started to strengthen relations 'with several neoliberal military dictatorships' (Fernández Jilberto and Hogenboom, 2010, p. 6). This was a major change in the relations between China and Latin America as previously the main objective of the Chinese was to create Red Flag or Revolutionary Communist Parties (like the infamous Sendero Luminoso [Shining Path] in Peru) and to critique social imperialism; all these contributed to the political and ideological divisions in Latin America after World War II.

In general, Latin America has welcomed these changes, probably based on the same economic pragmatism shown by other emerging economies. The current China's doctrine of the 'Four No's' (no hegemonism, no power politics, no arms races and no military alliances), proclaimed by President Hu Jintao in 2004, is seen in Latin America as favourable for strengthening mutual confidence, improving international cooperation and for preventing international confrontations (Fernández Jilberto and Hogenboom, 2010).

In this context, the official visits from heads of state between China and Latin America have increased as a result of a growing agenda full

Table 3.1 Number of visits by heads of state between China and Latin America

Year	China to Latin America	Latin America to China
2001	Chile, Argentina, Uruguay, Brazil, Venezuela, Cuba	Peru, Chile, Mexico, Venezuela
2002	Mexico (no official)[1]	Ecuador, Uruguay
2003		Ecuador, Cuba Guyana
2004	Chile, Brasil, Argentina, Cuba	Argentina, Brazil, Venezuela, Suriname
2005	Mexico	Peru, Colombia
2006		Venezuela, Bolivia
2007		Costa Rica
2008	Peru, Costa Rica, Cuba	Peru, Chile, Mexico, Brazil, Venezuela
2009		Chile, Brazil, Venezuela, Uruguay
2010	Brazil, Venezuela, Chile[2]	Peru[3], Argentina[4]

Notes:
From 2004 to 2011 the Chinese president visiting Latin America has been Hu Jintao; previously the visiting president was Jiang Zemin.
[1] President Jiang visit Mexico to attend the APEC annual meeting.
[2] These visits were cancelled due to the earthquake in Qinghai on April 14, 2010.
[3] President Alan Garcia from Peru postponed his official visit to China planned for April 2010.
[4] President Cristina Fernandez from Argentina cancelled her official visit to China planned for January, 2010.

Source: Based on data from Barcena and Rosales, 2010.

of mutual interests. **Table 3.1** presents details of these visits in the last ten years. President Chavez from the Bolivarian Republic of Venezuela has been one of the most frequent visitors to Beijing among his Latin American counterparts with five visits, followed by Peru's presidents Toledo and Garcia with a total of three visits (plus a postponed visit).

Trade

In commercial terms, the main consequence of these changes has been that in the first ten years of the twenty-first century, trade between China and Latin America has been most dynamic for both exports and imports. In fact, in the 2005–2009 period, the rate of growth of the trade between Latin American and China (in both directions, i.e., imports and exports) doubled the growth rate of the total Latin American and Chinese international trade. However, bilateral commerce still represents less than 10% of imports and exports for China and Latin America. This combination of high growth plus room to grow presents big challenges and opportunities for businesses on both sides (Barcena and Rosales, 2010). Table 3.2 presents GDP and exports performance for China and Latin America from 2003 to 2010.

Table 3.2 China and Latin America GDP and export volume growth 2003–2010

	GDP				Exports of goods and services			
	03–07	2008	2009	2010	03–07	2008	2009	2010
China (%)	11.0	9.6	9.1	10.5	20.4	13.9	–9.1	n/a
Latin America (%)	5.0	4.2	–1.9	5.2	7.5	1.1	–8.9	n/a

Note: n/a: not available.

Source: ECLAC, 2010b.

Table 3.3 presents a snapshot of the trade relationship between China and Latin America. In this table it can be seen that total exports from Latin America grew almost 19 times from 1995 to 2009, with an increase in primary products exports of 31 times and in manufacturing of only 12 times. Primary products (PP) exports from Mercosur grew more than 47 times during the same period (manufacturing only six times) and PP from other South American countries 17 times (manufacturing 45 times). On the other hand, total imports from China in the same period increased 32 times, with manufacturing being the most important part and PP growing 8 times only. Manufacturing imports to Mercosur increased 23 times and also 23 times to other South American countries (PP 5 and 12 times respectively). It is important to note that part of the increase in primary products exports may be explained by a price effect as most of the commodities exported by Latin America, especially by Mercosur, have experienced an important increase in their price (two, three, or four times in many cases).

A close look at **Table 3.3** shows that Mexico, Central America and the Caribbean have been suffering growing deficits since the early 1990s. This is because Mexico and Central American countries have a similar export basket to that of China and as a consequence they face strong competition in low and intermediate technology manufacturing and also in textiles and apparel (ECLAC, 2006). In fact, China has displaced Mexico as the United States' main trading partner mainly due to this.

On the other hand, South America is posting a relatively balanced situation (from surpluses until 2006). The sub-region appears as one of the most complementary trade partners for China (Lapper, 2007; Santiso, 2006a), they supply China with raw materials, food products and energy products to fuel its rapid growth, while Chinese companies find in South America a favourable growing market for their exports.

Table 3.3 Latin America's and the Caribbean's structure of merchandise trade with China, by category*

	Exports from Latin America to China											
	Total Latin America and the Caribbean				Mercosur				Other S. American countries			
	Primary Products	%	Manufactures	%	Primary Products	%	Manufactures	%	Primary Products	%	Manufactures	%
1995	847	35.0	1,574	65.0	373	23.1	1,240	76.9	467	67.1	229	32.9
1996	1,441	49.5	1,467	50.5	774	42.1	1,064	57.9	630	72.6	237	27.4
1997	1,836	55.0	1,504	45.0	1,015	48.8	1,064	51.2	799	72.9	297	27.1
1998	1,513	56.8	1,149	43.2	1,007	60.6	656	39.4	485	62.9	286	37.1
1999	1,198	56.2	933	43.8	666	53.5	579	46.5	519	75.8	166	24.2
2000	2,248	58.1	1,618	41.9	1,378	69.6	601	30.4	826	56.2	645	43.8
2001	2,983	56.5	2,293	43.5	2,072	66.0	1,066	34.0	856	52.6	771	47.4
2002	3,132	48.2	3,360	51.8	2,109	56.8	1,602	43.2	947	48.2	1,017	51.8
2003	4,991	44.4	6,244	55.6	3,590	50.4	3,534	49.6	1,226	43.1	1,619	56.9
2004	7,334	51.8	6,821	48.2	4,804	58.4	3,420	41.6	2,279	45.7	2,708	54.3
2005	11,195	58.9	7,810	41.1	6,927	68.1	3,244	31.9	3,982	55.9	3,138	44.1
2006	14,373	62.5	8,616	37.5	8,817	73.2	3,234	26.8	5,123	62.4	3,088	37.6
2007	18,417	55.3	14,864	44.7	11,262	70.1	4,814	29.9	6,725	47.6	7,389	52.4
2008	25,081	62.5	15,072	37.5	17,330	75.3	5,686	24.7	7,138	50.1	7,099	49.9
2009	25,979	57.5	19,236	42.5	17,404	72.2	6,713	27.8	7,859	43.5	10,212	56.5

Continued

Table 3.3 Continued

	Imports from China to Latin America											
	Total Latin America and the Caribbean				Mercosur				Other S. American countries			
	Primary Products	%	Manufactures	%	Primary Products	%	Manufactures	%	Primary Products	%	Manufactures	%
1995	80	3.2	2,379	96.8	42	3.9	1,016	96.1	15	1.9	776	98.1
1996	117	3.2	3,581	96.8	63	3.2	1,926	96.8	17	2.1	828	97.9
1997	126	2.6	4,788	97.4	58	2.4	2,323	97.6	28	2.5	1,081	97.5
1998	130	2.4	5,366	97.6	42	1.8	2,329	98.2	31	2.4	1,259	97.6
1999	245	4.2	5,559	95.8	46	2.3	1,973	97.7	47	3.8	1,209	96.2
2000	261	3.2	7,934	96.8	49	1.8	2,697	98.2	52	2.7	1,856	97.3
2001	311	3.0	10,093	97.0	75	2.7	2,687	97.3	44	1.8	2,436	98.2
2002	449	3.7	11,814	96.3	142	6.6	2,026	93.4	42	1.6	2,580	98.4
2003	378	2.2	16,872	97.8	133	4.1	3,084	95.9	52	1.6	3,219	98.4
2004	336	1.3	26,143	98.7	76	1.3	5,619	98.7	64	1.3	4,909	98.7
2005	477	1.4	34,507	98.6	110	1.4	7,645	98.6	69	1.0	6,557	99.0
2006	506	1.0	50,148	99.0	122	1.0	12,583	99.0	83	0.9	9,659	99.1
2007	518	0.9	59,316	99.1	149	0.8	17,430	99.2	85	0.7	11,800	99.3
2008	814	0.9	91,249	99.1	327	1.1	30,125	98.9	164	0.7	22,216	99.3
2009	645	0.8	77,899	99.2	213	0.9	23,882	99.1	175	1.0	17,776	99.0

Note: * Other South American countries: Bolivia, Chile, Colombia, Ecuador, Peru, Venezuela.
Source: ECLAC, 2011a.

Table 3.4 Evolution of trade between Latin America and China in the first semesters of 2009 and 2010 compared with the same period in the previous year

Exports		Imports	
January–June 2009	January–June 2010	January–June 2009	January–June 2010
–2.2%	44.8%	–18.0%	42.5%

Source: (ECLAC, 2010b).

As a consequence, China has become a major trading partner for Brazil, Chile, Argentina and Peru. In addition, China has obtained the market status economy from many of these countries (ECLAC, 2006).

The fact that they are complementary trade partners does not mean that there are no costs involved, in particular to Latin America. While the region is selling mainly commodities and raw materials, China is exporting low and medium technology products to a growing middle class in Latin American countries. These Chinese products may satisfy local consumers, but at the same time they threaten domestic producers. Also, the low production costs from China are hindering the possibilities of Latin American exports to other markets like the US or EU (ECLAC, 2005; Jenkins, 2008). In addition, exports from Latin America, in particular South America, may face competition from Asian economies especially those part of ASEAN (Association of South Asian Nations). Around 35% of exports from ASEAN to China potentially compete with products sold by Latin America (most of the remaining 65% are high technology manufacturers in which Latin America is not competing) (Fernández Jilberto and Hogenboom, 2010).

Table 3.4 presents the evolution of trade between Latin America and China in 2009 and 2010. In this table it is of particular interest how the trade between the two has quickly recovered from the consequences of the economic crisis, posting growth of more than 40% in the first six months of 2010.

Investments

There are two areas for analysis in terms of investments: (1) FDI from developed economies, and (2) bilateral investments between China and Latin America. For (1), an early work by the Inter-American Development Bank (IADB, 2004) on the impact of China on Latin America (using data up to 2002, just after the crises in Argentina and Brazil) hinted at tough competition for FDI from developed countries between the two regions. Also other works (Dussel Peters, 2005; Garcia-Herrero and Santabarbara, 2005) suggested that from 1995 to 2001 competition for funds from China had a negative impact on Latin American countries, especially on Mexico and Colombia. However, more recent studies have suggested that this competition has affected only Mexico and other countries in the Caribbean (Blazquez-Lidoy et al., 2006; Chantasasawat, Fung, Iizaka, and Siu, 2005; ECLAC, 2006). In this sense, Blazquez-Lidoy et al. (2006, p. 42) added that 'the 1990s golden years of the FDI rush towards Latin America might be over, at least until the processes of privatisation are not reopened, but at the same time Latin American countries are far from being left out of the map of FDI dynamics.'

Table 3.5 shows the FDI inward stock for China and selected Latin American and Caribbean countries since 1995. In this table it is possible to see that the stock of FDI in both regions has been growing steadily (14% for China and 15% for Latin America on average from 2005, with FDI stocks in Brazil growing at an average of 21.3% in the same period). It is also interesting to note that Latin America has a much higher percentage of FDI stock/GDP ratio at 36.5% in comparison with that of China (10.1%). The world's average FDI stock/GDP was 30.7% in 2009 (UNCTAD, 2010) which may hint that FDI to China still has more room to grow than FDI to Latin America.

For (2), bilateral investments between China and Latin America, they have been mainly in the China–Latin America direction. In fact, in the last years one of the main destinations of Chinese outward foreign direct investment (ODI) has been Latin America, with 50% of Chinese ODI in 2004 (more than the 30% that went towards Asia) (Blazquez-Lidoy et al., 2006, p. 35), with 53% in 2005, 40% in 2006 (MOFCOM, 2007) and with similar trends in 2008 (MOFCOM, 2008). In 2009, Latin America was the second destination for Chinese ODI after Hong Kong (MOFCOM, 2009a).

In this context, China has committed investments of around US $100 billion in the region before 2015 (La Nación, 2004d, 2004c; La Tercera, 2007a; Painter, 2008). There seem to be different reasons for these investments, like 'controlling assets and exerting political influence' (Lapper, 2005), securing the supply of natural resources to feed China's economic growth (Phillips, 2010), getting access to a market of almost 600 million and a $4 trillion economy for Chinese products (Fornes and Butt-Philip, 2011b; Shixue, 2007), or using tax havens as a stopover in their onward journey and, in some cases, to base their listing vehicles (Sutherland and Ning, 2011).

Table 3.5 FDI inward stock for China and selected Latin American and Caribbean countries, in billions of US dollars

	1995	1996	1997	1998	1999	2000	2001	2002	2003	2004	2005	2006	2007	2008	2009	Total	FDI stock as % of GDP 2009
China	102	128	154	175	186	193	203	217	228	245	272	293	327	378	473	3,795	10.1
Latin America and the Caribbean	187	225	298	369	429	502	577	553	629	732	817	934	1,162	1,260	1,473	10,875	36.5
South America	128	155	209	251	277	309	328	273	327	373	428	494	630	638	788	6,101	27.6
Argentina	28	34	42	48	62	68	80	43	48	53	55	60	68	77	81	924	26.2
Bolivia	2	2	2	3	4	5	6	7	5	5	5	5	5	6	6	75	37.0
Brazil	48	55	70	100	102	122	122	101	133	161	181	221	310	288	401	2,653	25.5
Chile	24	29	35	38	43	46	43	42	54	61	74	80	99	100	122	982	74.5
Colombia	6	12	20	17	13	11	15	18	21	25	37	45	56	67	74	458	32.8
Ecuador	4	4	5	6	6	6	7	8	9	9	10	10	11	12	12	129	21.7
Paraguay	1	1	1	1	1	1	1	1	1	1	1	2	2	2	3	23	17.8
Peru	6	7	8	8	10	11	12	13	13	13	16	20	27	32	37	242	29.1
Uruguay	1	1	1	2	2	2	2	1	2	2	3	4	6	9	10	53	31.5
Venezuela	8	10	25	29	31	35	39	39	41	42	45	46	44	44	41	547	12.2
Central America	48	56	67	78	95	115	161	186	205	232	256	281	316	347	365	3,006	36.2
Costa Rica	0	1	1	2	2	3	3	4	4	5	5	7	9	11	12	78	41.4
El Salvador	0	0	0	2	2	2	2	3	3	4	4	4	6	7	7	48	33.8
Guatemala	2	2	2	3	3	3	4	4	4	5	3	4	5	5	6	67	16.0
Honduras	1	1	1	1	1	1	2	2	2	2	3	4	4	5	6	37	40.5

Continued

Table 3.5 Continued

	1995	1996	1997	1998	1999	2000	2001	2002	2003	2004	2005	2006	2007	2008	2009	Total	FDI stock as % of GDP 2009
Mexico	41	47	56	64	78	97	140	164	181	204	227	247	274	297	310	2,588	35.4
Nicaragua	0	0	1	1	1	1	2	2	2	2	2	3	3	4	4	30	68.1
Panama	3	4	5	6	7	7	7	7	8	9	10	13	15	17	19	150	75.9
Caribbean	11	14	23	39	57	78	88	93	97	127	133	158	216	276	320	1,768	187.5
Bahamas	1	1	1	2	3	3	3	4	4	5	5	6	7	8	8	64	115.9
British Virgin Islands	1	2	6	14	22	32	36	37	40	58	49	56	85	129	156	725	n/a
Cayman Islands	3	4	7	11	18	26	30	29	27	36	47	58	81	87	98	571	n/a
Dominican Republic	–2	–2	–1	–1	1	2	3	4	4	4	5	6	8	11	13	46	28.5
Jamaica	2	2	2	2	3	3	4	4	5	6	7	8	9	10	11	83	89.9
Trinidad and Tobago	4	4	5	6	7	7	8	9	10	11	12	13	13	16	17	155	88.7

Source: UNCTAD, 2010.

Table 3.6 Chinese ODI to Latin America, per country, in millions of US dollars

	Chinese ODI stock – Dec 2008	Chinese ODI flows – Dec 2009	Chinese ODI stock – Est. Dec 2009	Stock in Latin America in % per country
World	184,000	43,300	220,000	
Latin America and the Caribbean	32,240	8,939	41,179	100 00
Cayman Islands	20,327	7,354	27,682	67 22
British Virgin Islands	10,477	1,330	11,807	28 67
Brazil	217	72	289	0 70
Peru	194	85	279	0 68
Argentina	173	39	213	0.52
Venezuela	156	20	176	0.43
Mexico	173	2	175	0.42
Ecuador	89	1	90	0.22
Panama	67	10	77	0.19
Cuba	72	–	72	0.17
Guyana	70	–	70	0.17
Surinam	68	–	68	0.16
Chile	58	5	63	0.15
Bolivia	29	5	34	0.08
Saint Vincent and Grenadines	32	–	32	0.08
Paraguay	5	15	20	0.05
Colombia	14	1	15	0.04
Granada	8	–	8	0.02
Barbados	3	–	3	0.01
Jamaica	2	–	2	0.01
Uruguay	2	–	2	0.01
Antigua and Barbuda	1	–	1	0.00
Trinidad and Tobago	1	–	1	0.00
Dominica	1	–	1	0.00
Bahamas	1	–	1	0.00
Belize	0	–	0	0.00
Dominican Republic	0	–	0	0.00
Honduras	–	–	–	–

Source: Barcena and Rosales, 2010; MOFCOM, 2009a.

Table 3.6 shows that most of Chinese ODI to Latin America is going to tax heavens as around 96% of these funds are heading to the Cayman Islands and the British Virgin Islands. The point is that data on ODI to tax havens do not count for an ultimate destination of an investment, only its immediate destination. In the Chinese case, this situation is particularly important 'owing to the widespread use of havens' (also encouraged until recently by preferential tax rates for foreign companies). The Cayman Islands and British Virgin Islands, owing in part to their historic links with Hong Kong, are favoured destinations for Chinese holding companies. In 2006, for example, the Cayman Islands actually became the largest recipient of Chinese ODI flows (with 44% of the total, exceeding even Hong Kong) (MOFCOM, 2008). The British Virgin Islands and Cayman Islands were the second and third largest holders of Chinese ODI stock in 2009, with 5.5% and 6.1% respectively (MOFCOM, 2010b). 'While a significant amount of this ODI may round-trip back to China, an unknown amount may also onward-journey to third countries' (Sutherland and Ning, 2011, p. 53).

In fact, a disaggregation of these figures shows that part of these funds seems to be then invested in projects in Latin America. This can be seen in Table 3.7, which shows that around US $17.3 billion of Chinese investments have headed to productive ventures in Latin American countries between 2003 and 2008.

On top of the investments listed in Table 3.7, other planned projects should be added. The 'super port' in Joao da Barra in Brazil, one of the largest in the world with an investment of US $2.56 billion, is one of the several ventures in which Chinese companies have been investing around $20 billion into the country in the first semester of 2010 (compared with a total of $83 million in 2009) (Phillips, 2010). Also in Brazil, the China Development Bank and Petrobras, the Brazilian oil company, signed a US $10 billion loan to guarantee the supply of 200,000 oil barrels per day to China for the next ten years. In addition, 'a recent study by Deloitte predicted that Chinese investments in Brazil could hit an average of about $40 billion a year between now and 2014, with companies throwing money at sectors ranging from telecommunications, infrastructure and farming, to oil, bio fuels, natural gas, mining and steel manufacturing' (Phillips, 2010).

These investments in 2010 join a projected US $1.7 billion hydro-electric dam along with US $1billion investments in oil exploration and infrastructure projects in Ecuador. Also US $1.4 billion invested in mining operations in Peru. But probably one of the most ambitious Chinese projects in Latin America is that of building an alternative to the Panama

Table 3.7 Chinese ODI to Latin America from 2003 to 2008, per country and sector, in millions of US dollars

	Sector	Investments 2003–2008
Argentina	Car industry, manufacture, distribution	
	Transport industry, manufacture	
Total		519
Bolivia	Metals, sales and commercialization	
Total		2
Brazil	Car industry, manufacture, distribution	
	Office machines and equipment, manufacture	
	Business services	
	Coal, oil, gas, extraction	
	Communications, manufacture, sales and training	
	Retail products	
	Financial services	
	Food and tobacco, sales and commercialization	
	Industrial machinery, tools and equipments, manufacture	
	Metals, extraction, manufacture	
	Transport industry, manufacture	
	Paper, printing and packaging, manufacture	
	Transport, logistics and distribution	
Total		8,548
Chile	Financial services	
	Industrial machinery, tools and equipment, manufacture	
Total		37
Colombia	Car industry, manufacture	
	Communications, training	
	Wood products, manufacture	
Total		242
Costa Rica	Coal, oil, gas, production	
Total		285
Cuba	Electronic appliances, manufacture	
Total		0
Ecuador	Coal, oil, gas, extraction, sales	
	Real estate	
Total		199
Guyana	Metals, manufacture	
Total		1,000
Mexico	Car industry, manufacture	

Continued

Table 3.7 Continued

	Sector	Investments 2003–2008
	Communications, R&D, training Electronic appliances, manufacture Industrial machinery, tools and equipment, sales, commercialisation Metals, extracts, manufacture Paper, printing and packaging, manufacture	
Total		**1,079**
Panama	Business services	
Total		**0**
Peru	Industrial machinery, tools and equipment, recycling Metals, extraction, sales, commercialisation	
Total		**4,555**
Uruguay	Car industry, manufacture	
Total		**100**
Venezuela	Office machines and equipment, manufacture Coal, oil, gas, extraction Communications, IT, internet infrastructure, manufacture Financial services Metals, extraction	
Total		**715**
Grand Total		**17,281**

Source: Barcena and Rosales, 2010.

Canal that would link Colombia's Atlantic and Pacific coasts by rail. 'The 220 km 'dry canal' would run from the Pacific to a new city near Cartagena where imported Chinese goods would be assembled for re-export throughout the Americas. Colombia-sourced raw materials would make the return journey to China' (Rathbone and Mapstone, 2011). Table 3.8 shows selected Chinese investments in Latin America to 2008.

These Chinese investments have not been without controversy in Latin America. Probably the most renowned one was the US $100 billion in investments committed by President Hu Jintao during his 2004 visit to the region; the Chinese government later corrected this to US $100 billion in bilateral trade (Painter, 2008). Then, it was found that many of the Chinese investments to Latin America were heading to the Cayman Islands and many questioned if they could be treated as real direct investments (Dyer and Lapper, 2007). There have been other issues related to relations with labour and care for the environment, especially in the extractive industries (Gutierrez, 2011). And finally, Chinese investments in Latin America have also been mentioned in the US Department of State communications leaked by Wikileaks in 2010; it seems that US officials in Beijing reported that many Latin American countries are sceptical of the real intentions of these Chinese investments in the region (Gutierrez, 2011).

For the future it is expected that the trade, and much of the ensuing investment, will continue growing. In addition, there is little that other states or groups of states can do about this, as the United States and the EU (most notably Spain) are preoccupied with resolving their financial and economic crises, and in emerging from them in reasonable order. They have neither the resources nor the will to challenge the élan of China's deepening interest in central and southern America.

As a result, China will acquire substantial soft power, politically as well as economically, as it settles down to be the major development partner of most Latin American states over the next decade. New roads, bridges, ports, telecoms infrastructure, financial services, refineries, mines and quarries will be the iconic results. The relationship with China for many Latin American states will be transformative – a source of 'concern' for the United States, as well as for some of the Latin American states who are themselves beneficiaries. The concerns are that such developments will meet the needs of China and Chinese investors, but will potentially also set back the more balanced development strategies of Latin American governments. And also concerns that the strongly bilateral character of these China–Latin American relations may prove to be incompatible with attempts to foster regional economic integration.

3.3 Main players

Latin America

Latin America has an area of approximately 21.7 million square km (7.9 square miles), almost 3.9% of the Earth's surface or 14.1% of its land surface area. As of 2010, its population was estimated at more than 590 million and its combined GDP at US $3.97 trillion (6.35 trillion at PPP) (CIA, 2011c). The Latin American expected economic growth rate is at about 5.7% for 2010 and 4% in 2011 (IMF, 2010). Latin America is the home of two of the world's largest economies in the world, Brazil and Mexico. There are a total of forty countries in Latin America and the Caribbean.

Table 3.8 Selected Chinese investments in Latin America to 2008, in millions of US dollars

Chinese Company	Project	Country	Estimated Amount	Type of investment
Sinopec	Construction of a gas pipeline linking South to Northeast	Brazil	1,000	JV with Petrobras
Baoshan Iron & Steel	Iron ore supply	Brazil	n/a	JV with Companhia Vale do Rio Doce
China Minmetals Corporation	Copper supply	Chile	n/a	JV with Codelco
Baosteel	Construction of a steel production plant in Maranhao	Brazil	1,500	JV with Companhia Vale do Rio Doce
Shougang Group	Iron ore	Peru	n/a	n/a
Huawei	Purchasing and selling agreements for the region	Latin America	n/a	Agreement with Spain's Telefonica
Zhu hai GREE	Air conditioning plant	Brazil	n/a	n/a
Sinosteel	Mining	Brazil	n/a	JV
CITIC Group	Construction of railways	Brazil	n/a	n/a
CNOOC	Oil exploration	Venezuela	n/a	JV with PDVSA
China Agribusiness Dev Trust & Investment Co	Inversiones Cadtic Ltda	Chile	38	New company: investments
Citifor	Citifor Chile Holdings Ltda	Chile	14	New company: forestry
Sun Kung Enterprise	Golden Spring Forestal	Chile	14	New company: forestry
China National Machinery & Equipment	Maquinaria China Limitada	Chile	0.6	New company: trade
Winning Streak Investment Ltd	Inversiones Misaki SA	Chile	5	New company: investments
Transworld produce	Sociedad Agricola Iglesia Colorada Ltda	Chile	0.5	Acquisition: agriculture
Zhizhong Wang	Forestal Minfortune SA	Chile	0.4	New company: forestry

Continued

Table 3.8 Continued

Chinese Company	Project	Country	Estimated Amount	Type of investment
Nishi Properties Ltd	Nishi Chile Ltd	Chile	0.3	New company: fish farming
Sinopec and PetroChina	Andes Petroleum	Ecuador	1,420	Acquisition
Leng Cheng Mining	Hipasam	Argentina	40	Acquisition: mining (closed since 1992)

Source: Dyer and Lapper, 2007; Santiso, 2007; Brazil's External Affairs Ministry, Chile's Foreign Investments Committee, Argentina's Ministry of Economy and Production.

Particularly in the United States, the term Latin America refers to all of the Americas south of the United States. This grouping comprises English-speaking countries like Belize, Jamaica, Barbados, Trinidad and Tobago, Guyana, Antigua and Barbuda, St. Lucia, Dominica, Grenada, St. Vincent and the Grenadines and the Bahamas; French-speaking Haiti and Martinique, Guadeloupe, French Guiana; and the Dutch-speaking Netherlands Antilles, Aruba and Suriname. This definition is based on a similar socioeconomic history characterised by formal or informal colonialism.

On the other hand, the United Nations geo scheme divides the Americas into (1) North America, and (2) Latin America and the Caribbean. The latter also comprises all the countries south of the US border (including Mexico as part of Central America) (UN Data, 2011). Both definitions are used indistinctly in this book. Figure 3.1 shows a map of Latin America including political divisions and main cities.

Spanish and Portuguese are the predominant languages of Latin America. Portuguese is spoken only in Brazil, the biggest and most populous country in the region. Spanish is the official language of most of the rest of the countries on the Latin American mainland, as well as in Puerto Rico (where it is co-official with English), Cuba and the Dominican Republic. French is spoken in Haiti and in the French overseas departments of Guadeloupe, Martinique, French Guiana, Saint Pierre and Miquelon. Dutch is the official language in Suriname, Aruba and the Netherlands Antilles. Native American languages are widely spoken in Peru, Guatemala, Bolivia, Paraguay and to a lesser degree, in Mexico, Panama, Ecuador and Chile. The vast majority of Latin Americans are Christians, mostly Roman Catholics (CIA, 2011c).

Figure 3.1 Map of Latin America
Source: CIA, 2011c.

Latin American countries participate in different trade agreements. The most important trade bloc is the Mercosur/Mercosul[2] (Mercado Común del Sur in Spanish, Mercado Comum do Sul in Portuguese, or Southern Common Market in English). Mercosur was founded in 1991 by Argentina, Brazil, Paraguay and Uruguay, which remain as full members; then Bolivia, Chile, Colombia, Ecuador, Peru and Venezuela joined as associate members, and Mexico as observer. Mercosur's main

MERCOSUR MERCOSUL

Figure 3.2 Mercosur logo
Source: Mercosur, 2011.

COMUNIDAD ANDINA
SECRETARIA GENERAL

Figure 3.3 CAN logo
Source: CAN, 2011.

purpose is to promote free trade and the fluid movement of goods, people and currency in the region (Mercosur, 2011).

A second trade agreement is the Comunidad Andina de Naciones (CAN – Andean Community of Nations in English)[3] formed by Bolivia, Chile, Colombia, Ecuador and Peru in 1969 under the name of Pacto Andino (Andean Pact in English). Venezuela joined in 1973. Then in

Figure 3.4 CARICOM logo
Source: CARICOM, 2011.

1976 Chile left the association and Venezuela followed suit in 2006. The CAN accepted Argentina, Brazil, Paraguay and Uruguay as associate members in 2005 to reciprocate the actions of Mercosur, which granted associated membership to all the Andean Community nations. Chile rejoined the CAN also as an associate member in 2006. The Mercosur and the CAN signed a free trade agreement in 2004 (BBC Mundo, 2004).

The Caribbean Community and Common Market (CARICOM)[4] was established in 1973, and it currently has 15 full members (Antigua and Barbuda, The Bahamas, Barbados, Belize, Dominica, Grenada, Guyana, Haiti, Jamaica, Montserrat, Saint Lucia, St. Kitts and Nevis, St. Vincent and the Grenadines, Suriname, Trinidad and Tobago) and 5 associate members (Anguilla, Bermuda, British Virgin Islands, Cayman Islands, Turks and Caicos Islands).

There are also minor blocs or trade agreements among Latin American countries. In 1995, Colombia, Mexico and Venezuela signed the G3 Free Trade Agreement (from which Venezuela withdrew in 2006). In 2004, the United States and the Central American countries of Costa Rica, El Salvador, Guatemala, Honduras and Nicaragua signed the Central America Free Trade Agreement (CAFTA); later in 2004, the Dominican Republic joined the negotiations and the agreement was renamed DR-CAFTA.[5]

Finally, a major development in South American economic integration took place in 2008 with the signing of the Constitutive Treaty of the UNASUR[6] (Unión de Naciones Suramericanas in Spanish, União de Nações Sul-Americanas – UNASUL in Portuguese, Union of South American Nations in English) in Brasilia, Brazil's capital. The UNASUR members are Argentina, Bolivia, Brazil, Chile, Colombia, Ecuador, Guyana, Paraguay, Peru, Suriname, Uruguay and Venezuela (i.e., all South American countries with the exception of Trinidad and Tobago, the French overseas department of French Guiana, and the British overseas territories of the Falkland Islands and the South Georgia and

Figure 3.5 UNASUR logo
Source: UNASUR, 2011.

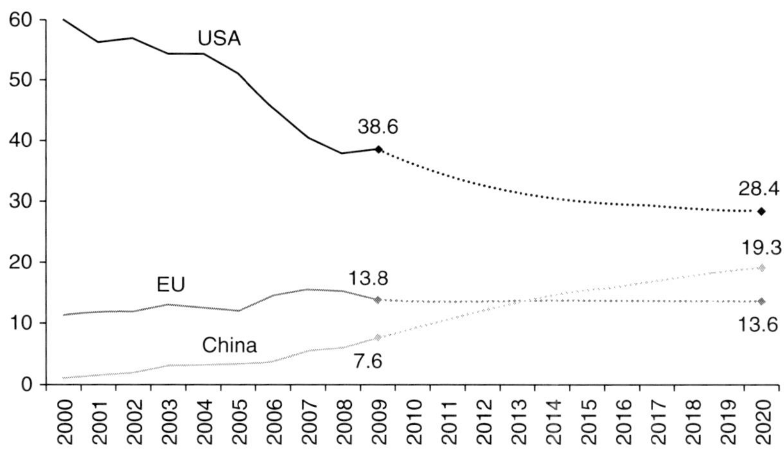

Figure 3.6 Latin American and the Caribbean exports to the main three destinations, 2000–2020 (projected), in percentage
Source: Barcena and Rosales, 2010.

South Sandwich Islands; the latter British territories are claimed by Argentina). The UNASUR is an intergovernmental union that integrates the Mercosur and the CAN modelled on the European Union.

One of UNASUR's main objectives is the creation of a single market of around 400 million consumers with the elimination of tariffs for non-sensitive products by 2014 and for sensitive products by 2019. UNASUR is also working in other areas like economic development, defence policy, infrastructure cooperation and free movement of people. After the

Table 3.9 Latin American and the Caribbean trade with China, rest of Asia, US, EU, and rest of the World, in percentage

Exports	**1990**	**1991**	**1992**	**1993**	**1994**	**1995**	**1996**	**1997**	**1998**	**1999**	**2000**	**2001**	**2002**	**2003**	**2004**	**2005**	**2006**	**2007**	**2008**	**2009**
China	0.7	0.8	0.8	0.9	0.9	1.1	1.2	1.2	1.0	0.7	1.1	1.6	1.9	3.0	3.0	3.3	3.4	4.8	4.7	6.8
Rest of Asia	8.5	8.7	6.5	6.0	6.4	6.4	5.6	4.9	3.6	4.1	3.4	3.0	2.8	1.9	1.7	1.8	2.0	1.7	1.4	7.5
US	39.3	36.2	44.9	46.8	46.7	46.3	48.5	48.8	51.9	57.3	58.4	55.6	56.8	54.3	53.3	50.1	48.8	44.7	41.5	39.7
EU	24.6	24.5	20.3	17.3	17.6	16.6	14.8	14.0	14.4	13.5	11.8	12.1	12.1	13.1	12.8	12.3	13.2	14.6	14.1	12.8
Rest of the World	27.3	30.1	27.9	29.2	28.6	29.9	30.2	31.3	29.3	24.6	25.6	27.9	26.6	28.0	29.3	32.8	32.9	34.4	38.6	33.2
Imports	**1990**	**1991**	**1992**	**1993**	**1994**	**1995**	**1996**	**1997**	**1998**	**1999**	**2000**	**2001**	**2002**	**2003**	**2004**	**2005**	**2006**	**2007**	**2008**	**2009**
China	0.6	0.5	0.6	0.8	0.8	1.1	1.5	1.6	1.7	1.9	2.3	2.9	3.7	5.0	6.5	7.1	8.6	9.4	10.9	11.7
Rest of Asia	8.2	8.8	8.4	8.8	9.7	8.8	7.8	7.9	7.9	7.1	6.6	7.4	7.2	5.6	4.9	5.1	4.0	3.0	1.3	12.8
US	40.2	40.9	47.9	46.8	44.4	43.4	44.7	45.5	46.9	49.4	48.8	46.2	45.3	43.2	38.8	36.6	34.3	33.2	31.6	29.2
EU	20.4	19.8	17.2	17.3	18.5	18.5	17.6	17.2	17.5	16.8	14.0	15.0	14.6	14.6	14.3	14.3	13.4	13.6	14.0	13.8
Rest of the World	31.3	30.5	26.3	26.8	27.1	28.6	29.0	28.2	26.5	25.3	28.7	28.9	29.7	32.0	35.8	37.5	40.2	41.2	42.7	32.4

Source: Barcena and Rosales, 2010.

signing of the treaty, Brazil's then President Luiz Inacio Lula da Silva said UNASUR shows that South America was becoming a 'global player' (BBC, 2008).

The following tables present Latin America and the Caribbean's trade with China and the rest of the world.

Table 3.9 shows that since 2000 China has been increasing its share while the United States has seen a decrease in its trade with the region. It also shows that the Rest of Asia is becoming an important trade partner for Latin America. Figures 3.6 and 3.7 present the projected Latin American trade with the main three destinations and sources. In these figures, and complementing what Table 3.9 shows, it is possible to see that the United States' share of trade with Latin America will decrease substantially, and that it is expected that China will overtake the EU as the second largest trade partner of Latin America in 2014 or 2015.

Table 3.10 presents the evolution of Latin American exports to main destinations as a percentage of total exports. In this table it is possible to see that China has increased more than 10% its relative participation as an export destination for most Latin American countries in the period 2000 to 2009. It is also possible to see that this growth has been mainly at the expense of the United States and EU. This table also shows that the intratrade in Central America and the Caribbean has grown more than 10%, probably a consequence of the DR-CAFTA.

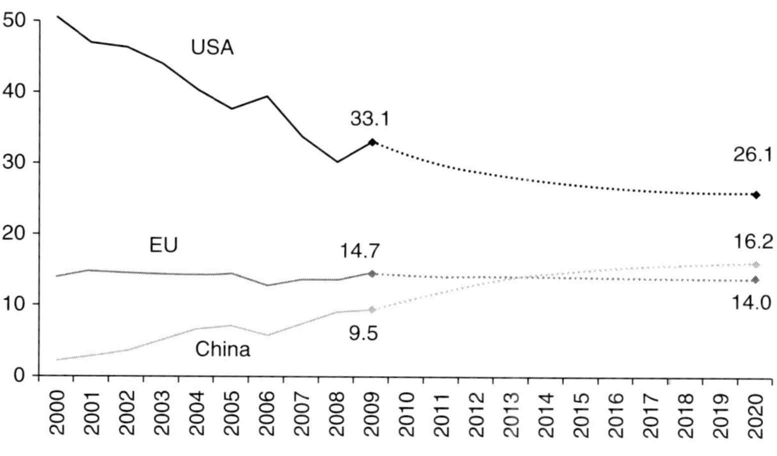

Figure 3.7 Latin American and the Caribbean imports from the main three sources, 2000–2020 (projected), in percentage

Source: Barcena and Rosales, 2010.

Table 3.10 Evolution of Latin American and the Caribbean exports to main destinations, in percentage of total exports

		China		Asia Pacific		US		UE 27		Latin America and the Caribbean	
		2000	2009	2000	2009	2000	2009	2000	2009	2000	2009
South America	Argentina	3.0	6.6	9.4	15.3	12.0	6.2	18.0	18.6	48.1	42.2
	Bolivia	0.4	2.5	1.4	18.5	24.0	7.7	17.3	9.1	44.2	59.9
	Brazil	2.0	13.2	10.3	26.1	24.3	10.2	28.0	22.2	24.8	20.1
	Chile	5.0	23.2	26.1	46.1	16.5	11.3	25.2	19.6	21.9	19.1
	Colombia	0.2	2.9	2.6	6.0	50.4	39.7	13.9	14.2	28.9	24.6
	Ecuador	1.2	0.9	10.9	2.6	37.9	33.5	12.9	15.0	31.5	42.6
	Paraguay	0.7	1.1	2.0	1.1	3.9	1.8	13.6	16.0	74.5	75.1
	Peru	6.4	15.4	16.9	26.9	28.0	16.3	22.0	15.6	18.1	14.9
	Uruguay	4.0	4.3	8.3	8.5	8.3	3.3	16.3	15.1	54.2	39.9
	Venezuela	0.1	2.9	1.9	7.6	59.6	48.8	5.8	9.4	19.6	10.4
Central America	Costa Rica	0.2	8.8	5.5	17.7	52.0	35.8	22.1	17.4	19.0	27.3
	El Salvador	0.0	0.1	0.4	2.8	65.5	46.6	5.7	5.8	27.8	43.5
	Guatemala	0.1	0.4	3.6	3.2	44.0	42.5	10.9	5.5	35.6	40.1
	Honduras	0.0	1.5	1.6	4.7	79.3	40.7	4.5	23.0	6.0	29.8
	Mexico	0.2	0.6	1.4	2.4	88.2	87.6	3.5	3.8	3.6	3.2
	Nicaragua	0.0	–	0.8	2.5	57.2	29.5	16.4	13.3	23.4	68.1
	Panama	0.2	2.5	2.0	8.2	45.9	42.6	21.7	24.1	33.2	19.3

Caribbean	Bahamas	0.0	0.0	2.4	24.6	48.3	33.7	29.8	24.7	1.5	10.5
	Barbados	–	0.4	0.7	1.1	13.5	7.5	18.5	12.4	16.2	75.8
	Belize	–	0.0	0.8	7.0	45.0	30.3	27.8	37.3	30.6	12.2
	Cuba	4.8	26.4	9.8	29.9	–	–	38.5	20.9	10.5	19.1
	Dominican Republic	–	2.0	1.4	4.3	91.1	61.9	6.3	10.4	4.2	20.7
	Dominica	–	0.7	0.0	30.1	10.9	1.8	56.9	26.3	28.8	37.9
	Grenada	–	0.0	3.1	0.7	7.4	12.9	56.2	7.8	24.4	74.1
	Guyana	–	1.0	6.6	3.9	20.5	15.6	48.5	25.1	10.3	18.6
	Haiti	–	0.7	1.2	2.5	83.0	78.7	12.5	3.7	6.5	9.6
	Jamaica	0.0	1.1	1.0	5.5	28.4	38.2	31.8	21.1	5.1	9.1
	St Kitts y Nevis	–	0.0	3.3	0.5	61.3	62.7	34.2	4.5	3.8	13.1
	St Lucia	–	0.0	0.1	21.3	16.6	9.3	68.9	46.0	8.7	22.1
	St Vincent and the Grenadines	–	0.4	0.0	5.7	10.6	0.5	54.6	74.9	34.0	17.2
	Suriname	–	0.5	6.2	1.2	11.8	9.9	38.3	24.2	6.3	9.3
	Trinidad and Tobago	0.1	0.7	1.4	4.4	53.9	36.3	9.0	18.2	18.0	36.9
Latin America and the Caribbean		**1.0**	**6.9**	**5.0**	**14.6**	**59.7**	**40.1**	**11.1**	**13.9**	**16.3**	**17.7**

Notes: Increase in the relative participation of the destination over the total exported (> 10%)

Reduction in the relative participation of the destination over the total exported (> 10%)

Source: Barcena and Rosales, 2010.

Table 3.11 China's position as a trade partner for selected Latin American countries

	Exports		Imports	
	2000	2008	2000	2008
Argentina	6	2	4	3
Bolivia	12	10	8	6
Brazil	12	1	11	2
Chile	5	1	4	2
Colombia	35	4	15	2
Costa Rica	26	2	16	3
Ecuador	13	9	10	2
El Salvador	35	16	18	5
Guatemala	30	18	15	4
Honduras	35	11	18	7
Mexico	25	5	6	3
Nicaragua	19	14	18	4
Panama	22	4	17	4
Paraguay	11	9	4	1
Peru	4	2	13	2
Uruguay	5	8	6	3
Venezuela	37	3	18	3

Source: Barcena and Rosales, 2010.

Table 3.11 shows China's position as a trade partner for selected Latin American countries. In this table it can be seen that China is within the top three for almost all countries in the list with the exception of Bolivia, El Salvador, Guatemala, Honduras, Nicaragua and Panama.

On the other hand, the relationship with China has created threats and opportunities for Latin America. Within the threats it is possible to mention that: (1) the high demand for commodities can delay the diversification from extraction-based industries to value-added goods in some countries, potentially damaging future development options (Santiso, 2006a); (2) the Caribbean countries' share of the US textile market has been reduced mainly due to competition from China, although their proximity and preferential access are still relative advantages; (3) trade between Latin America and China in the last few years has been mainly an exchange of raw materials for manufactured goods (Sanchez Ancochea, 2006).

Potential opportunities for Latin America from the relationship with China worth mentioning are: (1) an important part of the region's real GDP growth in the last years can be attributed to China (Sanchez Ancochea, 2006); (2) China has been a great supporter of Brazil (and the

Group of 20) in the WTO, improving its bargaining power against the United States and the EU; (3) the increasing Chinese investments in the energy and infrastructure sectors have improved the host governments' bargaining power with other foreign investors, mainly Spanish companies; (4) the possibility of exploiting the region's comparative and competitive advantages in agriculture, opening new markets for products with restrictions (tariff barriers, non-tariff barriers, quotas, etc.) to enter the United States and the EU; (5) the expected flow of tourists from China where Latin America has an international comparative advantage (100 million Chinese tourists are expected by 2020 [IADB, 2004]); (6) access to the enormous Chinese domestic market; (7) policy cooperation in areas such as privatisation, regional integration, public services regulation, non-performing loan portfolios in banking, etc. (IADB, 2004); (8) the US $100,000 million in investments committed by China in much needed infrastructure across the region (for example, 'for most Latin American countries, transport costs are even greater barriers to US markets than import tariffs' (Blazquez-Lidoy et al., 2006, p. 23).

Box 3.1 presents a short description of the main Latin American countries.

Box 3.1 A short description of the main Latin American countries, in alphabetical order

Argentina[7]

Argentina (República Argentina) is the second largest country in South America after Brazil. It is a federal republic organised with 23 provinces plus the autonomous city of Buenos Aires, the country's capital. It is the eighth largest country in the world by land area and the largest among Spanish-speaking nations (although Mexico, Colombia and Spain are more populous). Argentina was part of the Spanish Crown's Viceroyalty of the Rio de la Plata until a revolution in 1810. The country then declared its independence in 1816.

Argentina is the third largest Latin American economy after Brazil and Mexico, but with one of the highest human developed index and GDP per capita in the region, and a relatively well educated labour force. The country had a period of continued growth and development mainly from 1880 to the end of World War II when it was the world's sixth largest economy. Since then, Argentina has been immersed in a series of political and economic cycles (including a war with the UK for the Falkland Islands/Islas Malvinas in 1982). Due mainly to this, the country has been described by many commentators as the superpower that never was (see for example (Beattie, 2009; Porter, 1990). Nevertheless, during the last decade Argentina has grown steadily, posting positive annual variations of around 5% on average since 2005. Argentina is the world's third largest producer of soybeans (after the United States and Brazil).

Figure 3.8 Argentina's flag and coat of arms

Brazil[8]

Brazil (República Federativa do Brasil) is the largest country in South America. It is a federal republic organised with 26 states plus a federal district where the capital city, Brasilia, is located. It is the world's fifth largest country both by geographical area and by population. It is the only Portuguese-speaking country in the Americas and the largest Portuguese-speaking country in the world. Brazil was a colony of Portugal from 1500 and then part of the UK with Portugal and the Algarves. In 1808, the capital of the kingdom was transferred to Rio de Janeiro when Napoleon invaded Portugal. Brazil became independent in 1822 as the Empire of Brazil. The country has been a federal republic since 1889.

Brazil is currently the world's fifth largest economy (Leahy, 2011b). It enjoyed a period of development and industrialisation during the 1960s and it has regained international presence since the beginnings of the twenty-first century mainly due to its importance in the commodities markets and its inclusion in the BRIC group of countries. Brazil will host the Football World Cup in 2014 and Rio de Janeiro, one of the country's most famous cities, will host the 2016 Olympic Games. Brazil is the world's second largest producer of soybean (after the United States).

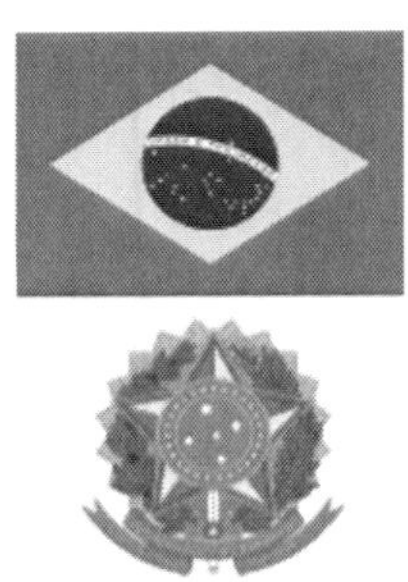

Figure 3.9 Brazil's flag and coat of arms

Chile[9]

Chile (República de Chile) is located in the Southwest of South America in a narrow coastal strip between the Andes Mountains and the Pacific Ocean. It is a republic divided into 15 regions. The capital city Santiago is located in the Región Metropolitana. Chile was part of the Spanish Crown's Viceroyalty of Peru until a change of regime in 1810. It was declared independent in 1818.

Chile is currently one of South America's most stable and prosperous nations. It leads Latin American nations in human development, competitiveness, income per capita, globalisation, economic freedom and low perception of corruption (UNDP, 2010). In 2005, Chile was the first Latin American country to sign a Free Trade Agreement with China (China Daily, 2005) (see Appendix 4), and then in 2010 Chile became the first South American country to join the Organisation for Economic Co-operation and Development (OECD). Chile is the world's largest copper producer.

Figure 3.10 Chile's flag and coat of arms

Colombia[10]

Colombia (República de Colombia) has the second largest population in South America after Brazil and it has the fourth largest economy in Latin America. It is a republic divided into 32 departments and one capital district. The capital city is Bogota. Colombia from 1499 was part of the Spanish Crown's Viceroyalty of New Granada until 1819 when it won independence from Spain. Then the Republic of Colombia was declared in 1886 from which Panama seceded in 1903.

Colombia developed rapidly during the twentieth century but this was not enough to avoid finishing the century with one of the worst wealth distributions in the world, which was aggravated by cocaine trade-fuelled armed conflicts in the 1980s. In the last decade violence has decreased dramatically (BBC, 2011a) and the economy has grown steadily, mainly based on commodities exports. Due to these improvements *BusinessWeek* named Colombia as one of 'the most extreme emerging market on Earth' (Farzad, 2007).

Figure 3.11 Colombia's flag and coat of arms

Costa Rica[11]

Costa Rica (República de Costa Rica) is the only Latin American country included in the list of the world's 22 older democracies and it has been ranked third in the world, and first among the Americas, in terms of the 2010 Environmental Performance Index. It is a republic divided into seven provinces. The capital city is San José. Costa Rica was part of the Spanish Crown's Viceroyalty of New Spain until 1821 when it became independent. Costa Rica was then part of the Mexican Empire and then of the Federal Republic of Central America until 1838 when it proclaimed itself sovereign.

'The traditional agricultural exports of bananas, coffee, sugar, and beef are still the backbone of commodity export trade, a variety of industrial and specialized agricultural products have broadened export trade in recent years. High value added goods and services, including microchips, have further bolstered exports. Tourism continues to bring in foreign exchange, as Costa Rica's impressive biodiversity makes it a key destination for ecotourism. Foreign investors remain attracted by the country's political stability and relatively high education levels, as well as the fiscal incentives offered in the free trade zones; and Costa Rica has attracted one of the highest levels of foreign direct investment per capita in Latin America' (CIA, 2011a). Costa Rica was the third Latin American country to sign a FTA with China (see Appendix 6).

Figure 3.12 Costa Rica's flag and coat of arms

Ecuador[12]

The diversity in natural species makes Ecuador (República del Ecuador) one of the 17 most diverse countries in the world. It is a republic divided into 24 provinces. The capital city is Quito. Ecuador was part of the northern Inca Empire until 1533 when it was conquered by the Spanish. From 1717 it was part of the Spanish Crown's Viceroyalty of New Granada until 1822 when it became independent. Since then the country went through different periods of political and economic instability, including a series of armed conflicts with its neighbours. Ecuador returned to democratic rule at the end of the 1970s. In 2008, the country approved its twentieth constitution since gaining independence.

'Ecuador is substantially dependent on its petroleum resources, which have accounted for more than half of the country's export earnings and approximately one-third of public sector revenues in recent years' (CIA, 2011d). In addition, it has a rich agriculture with important exports of bananas, flowers, coffee, cacao, sugar, tropical fruits, palm oil, palm hearts, rice, roses and corn. Ecuador is one of the smallest members of the Organization of Petroleum Exporting Countries (OPEC), and one of the two Latin American members along with Venezuela.

Figure 3.13 Ecuador's flag and coat of arms

Mexico[13]

Mexico (Estados Unidos Mexicanos) has the second largest population and it is also the second largest economy in Latin America after Brazil. It is the most populous Spanish-speaking country in the world. It is a federal republic divided into 31 states and a federal district. The capital is Mexico City (Distrito Federal or simply DF in Spanish). From 1521 Mexico was part of the Spanish Crown's Viceroyalty of New Spain until 1821 when its independence was recognised by Spain. Since then the country navigated through a period of economic and political instability that finished in 1910 with the Mexican Revolution. The current political system started in 1917 with the promulgation of the Constitution.

Mexico is within the top 13 world's largest economies and is expected to be the fifth in years to come (Goldman Sachs, 2010). In 1994, Mexico was the first Latin American country to join the OECD. Most of the country's economic development in the last 20 years has been based on the links with the United States and Canada within the North America Free Trade Agreement (NAFTA). Around 50% of its exports and 45% of its imports go/come to/from these two countries. Mr Carlos Slim from Mexico has been named the richest man in the world by Forbes magazine (Kroll and Miller, 2010)

Figure 3.14 Mexico's flag and coat of arms

Peru[14]

Peru (República del Perú) was home to one of the world's oldest civilisations, the Norte Chico and then the Inca Empire. It is a republic divided into 25 regions and the province of Lima, the latter being the capital city. From 1542 Peru was part of the Spanish Crown's Viceroyalty of Peru until 1821 when it became independent. Since independence the country went through a long period of economic and political instability. Peru returned to democratic leadership in 1980.

Peru's export-oriented economy has been one of the world's top performers with an average annual positive variation of more than 6% since 2002. The country's economy is based mainly on natural resources exports, which makes it vulnerable to price fluctuations and economic cycles. Peru signed a Free Trade Agreement with China in 2009, the second Latin American country to sign such an agreement with China after Chile (see Appendix 5). Peru is the world's third largest producer of copper (after Chile and the United States).

Figure 3.15 Peru's flag and coat of arms

Venezuela[15]

Venezuela (República Bolivariana de Venezuela) is considered a country with extremely high biodiversity. It is a federal republic with 23 states, a federal dependency, and a capital district where Caracas, the capital city, can be found. From 1522 Venezuela was part of the Spanish Crown's Viceroyalty of New Granada until 1811 when it was the first Spanish American colony to declare independence (it then achieved full independence from Gran Colombia in 1830). After independence, the country was ruled mainly by military strongmen (caudillos in Spanish); it first saw democratic rule from 1945 to 1948 and after a period of dictatorship it has remained democratic since 1958.

Venezuela's economy is heavily dominated by oil; the sector represents around 35% of the country's GDP, around 80% of its exports, and around 50% of the government's income. Venezuela is a founding member of the OPEC. The main destination of its oil exports is the United States; the second is China.

Figure 3.16 Venezuela's flag and coat of arms

Table 3.12 Net foreign direct investments to selected Latin American countries, by country of origin, in millions of US dollars

	1999	2000	2001	2002	2003	2004	2005	2006	2007	2008	2009
Argentina											
The Netherlands	424	378	1302	−436	−170	983	1057	107	576	808	n/a
United States	1307	947	533	342	−251	618	1249	860	837	1616	n/a
France	1536	656	521	−624	−185	389	220	−83	571	−26	n/a
Germany	272	69	−100	381	112	336	69	268	490	411	n/a
Chile	201	96	−245	22	24	171	611	508	469	824	n/a
Others	20244	8273	155	2464	2121	1777	3459	6025	4720	5913	n/a
Brazil											
United States	8088	5399	4465	2615	2383	3978	4644	4434	6039	7047	4902
Luxembourg	290	1027	285	1013	239	747	139	745	2855	5937	537
The Netherlands	2042	2228	1892	3372	1445	7705	3208	3495	8116	4639	6515
Japan	5702	9593	827	504	1368	243	779	648	465	4099	1673
Spain	2115	2035	2767	587	710	1055	1220	1514	2164	3851	3424
Others			10807	10687	6757	6538	11531	11396	14066	18884	14629
Chile											
Canada	518	744	142	913	188	368	84	1833	334	2190	88
United States	1389	788	1808	551	373	123	−15	337	266	550	2848
Spain	4620	643	366	248	160	3742	207	75	107	627	43
Japan	251	55	145	58	31	18	47	51	33	386	258
Mexico	72	2	14	3	16	150	605	47	55	247	87
Others	2380	807	2525	1608	518	235	870	825	578	1243	1759

Colombia												
	United States	545	120	223	784	274	874	1410	1524	1389	1745	2314
	Panama	180	259	129	40	135	10	208	240	477	760	203
	Spain	154	479	161	107	155	136	599	492	289	564	–327
	Mexico	6	23	12	21	19	16	1063	31	340	412	337
	UK	18	1	14	–11	35	16	3747	17	35	200	386
	Others	1427	2384	1134	739	561	914	1112	870	1364	1650	–243
Costa Rica												
	United States	n/a	280	257	328	354	557	532	695	940	1218	747
	Mexico	n/a	29	33	31	38	29	37	31	64	112	73
	Spain	n/a	22	26	0	7	7	14	10	54	76	50
	Germany	n/a	10	3	1	58	16	7	25	59	60	39
	El Salvador	n/a	15	16	23	25	14	21	33	41	54	35
	Others	n/a	53	125	275	92	171	250	674	738	501	378
Ecuador												
	Mexico	n/a	n/a	n/a	0	6	0	7	43	–40	598	–3
	Spain	n/a	n/a	n/a	1	3	1	3	7	85	384	770
	Panama	n/a	n/a	n/a	39	85	94	76	67	77	192	589
	China	n/a	n/a	n/a	16	20	–8	–20	12	85	59	172
	Canada	n/a	n/a	n/a	0	19	274	29	–252	49	57	73
	Others	n/a	n/a	n/a	727	739	477	398	395	–61	1064	558
Mexico												
	United States	7485	12920	21411	13013	9190	8619	11638	12431	11577	8938	5811
	Spain	1042	2113	2887	4960	2885	7854	1190	1592	5200	4322	630
	Canada	693	670	1031	233	303	551	450	539	659	2361	1034
	UK	–188	283	126	1254	1074	274	1310	1261	565	1387	428
	The Netherlands	1087	2721	2653	1557	715	3341	2437	2742	4363	1158	1461
	Others	3725	–678	1694	2706	2309	3020	4897	750	4913	3785	2054

Continued

Table 3.12 Continued

		1999	2000	2001	2002	2003	2004	2005	2006	2007	2008	2009
Peru												
	Chile	n/a	n/a	106	15	1	–125	–82	62	32	591	181
	Italy	n/a	n/a	202	124	–216	103	–504	65	–22	414	0
	South Africa	n/a	n/a	49	603	3	0	268	467	0	405	0
	Norway	n/a	n/a	117	0	0	25	5	15	0	276	0
	France	n/a	n/a	3	29	18	0	0	0	–30	148	4
	Others	n/a	n/a	308	240	249	–120	904	904	341	311	588
Venezuela												
	Spain	n/a	478	214	89	83	84	40	274	295	237	n/a
	The Netherlands	n/a	–10	78	117	56	304	53	–74	203	84	n/a
	Panama	n/a	42	44	20	23	29	38	29	53	29	n/a
	Colombia	n/a	–38	3	5	–8	1	2	9	22	3	n/a
	Others	n/a	4227	3338	561	1893	1087	2474	–832	76	1363	n/a

Source: ECLAC, 2010a.

Table 3.12 presents the net foreign direct investment received by the Latin American countries listed in Box 3.1. As can be seen in this table, US companies continue to be the main foreign investors in most of the countries (Argentina, Brazil, Colombia, Costa Rica and Mexico) followed by European firms (Spanish companies are the largest investors in Chile, Ecuador and Venezuela). Unfortunately the information presented by ECLAC (the UN's Economic Commission for Latin America and the Caribbean) is still not disaggregating China (except in Ecuador) as a stand-alone foreign investor probably because Chinese investments are a relatively new phenomenon. However, comparing the figures in this table with those in Table 3.6 and Table 3.7 (both presenting official data also from ECLAC) it is possible to see that the 'others' line, presumably the line in which Chinese investments are considered, has been growing steadily in the last three to four years overtaking in most of the countries (except Mexico and Costa Rica) the FDI from American and/or European investors.

China[16]

China (People's Republic of China – 中华人民共和国) is the most populous state in the world with more than 1.3 billion people. Located in East Asia, it is a single-party state governed by the Communist Party of China (CPC). China is divided into 22 provinces, 5 autonomous regions (Xinjiang, Inner Mongolia, Tibet, Ningxia and Guangxi), 4 directly administered municipalities (Beijing, Tianjin, Shanghai and Chongqing) and 2 highly autonomous special administrative regions (SARS) (Hong Kong and Macau). Beijing is the capital city. It is the third or fourth largest country by total area (the first is Russia, second is Canada, and third or fourth is the United States; fifth comes Brazil) depending on the definition of what is included in this total.

In 2010, China became the world's second largest economy overcoming Japan (IMF, 2011). But being an economic superpower is not new for China: in 18 of the last 20 centuries the country has had the largest economy in the world. In the later part of the Qing dynasty China's economic development began to slow and Europe's rapid development during and after the Industrial Revolution enabled it to surpass China (Dahlman and Aubert, 2001). The economy of ancient China introduced to the world a number of economic concepts, like the use of coins and money, land distribution for non-aristocrats and the development of a merchant class.

Since the introduction of market-based economic reforms in 1978 (see Box 3.2), China has become the world's fastest growing major economy, the world's largest exporter and the second largest importer of goods (BBC, 2011b). China is a permanent member of the United Nations Security Council and also a member of formal/informal multilateral organisations like the WTO, APEC, BRIC, Shanghai Cooperation Organisation and G20.

Box 3.2 A short description of the People's Republic of China

'People in China take pride in calling themselves the offspring of Huang Di or Yellow Emperor, a tribal chief who dwelled in the Yellow River Valley more than four millenniums ago. Pre-historical legends about the Yellow Emperor and other outstanding personages of his time abound in ancient Chinese books. Legend has it that the Yellow Emperor made weapons out of jade to conquer other tribes, while his wife, Lei Zu, introduced the rearing of silkworms. The Yellow Emperor taught tribesmen to domesticate wild animals and to grow cereals, and as a result his tribes grew in strength and defeated the tribes under Yan Di (Emperor Yan). Later, the Yellow Emperor and Emperor Yan formed an alliance that conquered all the other tribes in the Yellow River Valley. Today the Yellow Emperor is regarded as the ancestor of the Chinese people, who call themselves the descendants of Yan Di and Huang Di (Emperor Yan and Yellow Emperor)' (Gov.cn, 2006).

Table 3.13 A brief chronology of the main Chinese dynasties and republics

Xia Dynasty	about 2070 BC–1600 BC
Shang Dynasty	about 1600 BC–1046 BC
Zhou Dynasty	about 1046 BC–221 BC
Western Zhou Dynasty	about 1046 BC–771 BC
Eastern Zhou Dynasty	770BC–256BC
Spring and Autumn Period	770BC–476BC
Warring States	475BC–221BC
Qin Dynasty	221BC–206BC
Han Dynasty	202BC–220AD
Western Han	202BC–8AD
Eastern Han	25AD–220AD
Three Kingdoms	220AD–280AD
Wei	220AD–265AD
Shu	221AD–263AD
Wu	222AD–280AD
Jin Dynasty	265AD–420AD
Western Jin Dynasty	265AD–316AD
Eastern Jin Dynasty	317AD–420AD
Sixteen Kingdoms	304AD–439AD

Continued

Table 3.13 Continued

Northern and Southern Dynasties	386AD–589AD
Northern Dynasties	386AD–581AD
Southern Dynasties	420AD–589AD
Sui Dynasty	581AD–618AD
Tang Dynasty	618AD–907AD
Five Dynasties and Ten Kingdoms	907AD–979AD
Song Dynasty	960AD–1276AD
Northern Song Dynasty	960AD–1127AD
Southern Song Dynasty	1127AD–1276AD
Liao Dynasty	916AD–1125AD
Western Xia Dynasty	1038AD–1227AD
Jin Dynasty	1115AD–1234AD
Yuan Dynasty	1271AD–1368AD
Ming Dynasty	1368AD–1644AD
Qing Dynasty	1644AD–1911AD
Republic of China	1912AD–1949AD
People's Republic of China	founded on Oct.1, 1949

Source: Gov.cn, 2006

China is one of the world's oldest civilisations and a country with a long and rich history. The compass, gunpowder, the art of paper-making and block printing invented by the ancient Chinese have contributed to the progress of mankind. The Great Wall, Grand Canal and other projects built by the Chinese people are regarded as engineering feats in the world (Gov.cn, 2006).

The People's Republic of China was founded in 1949 under Mao Zedong leadership as chairman of the CPC. The country went through different economic and political cycles like The Great Leap Forward from 1958 to 1961 (aimed at rapidly transforming the country from an agrarian economy into a modern communist society through the process of agriculturalisation, industrialisation and collectivisation), the Great Proletarian Cultural Revolution (widely known as the Cultural Revolution) from 1966 to 1976 (led by Chairman Mao was 'a great political revolution in which one class would overthrow another' designed to further cement socialism in the country by removing capitalist elements from Chinese society (Gov.cn, 2006). 'After 1978, Mao's successor Deng Xiaoping and other leaders focused on market-oriented economic development and by 2000 output had quadrupled... China since the early 1990s has increased its global outreach and participation in international organizations' (CIA, 2011b).

Figure 3.17 China's flag and emblem

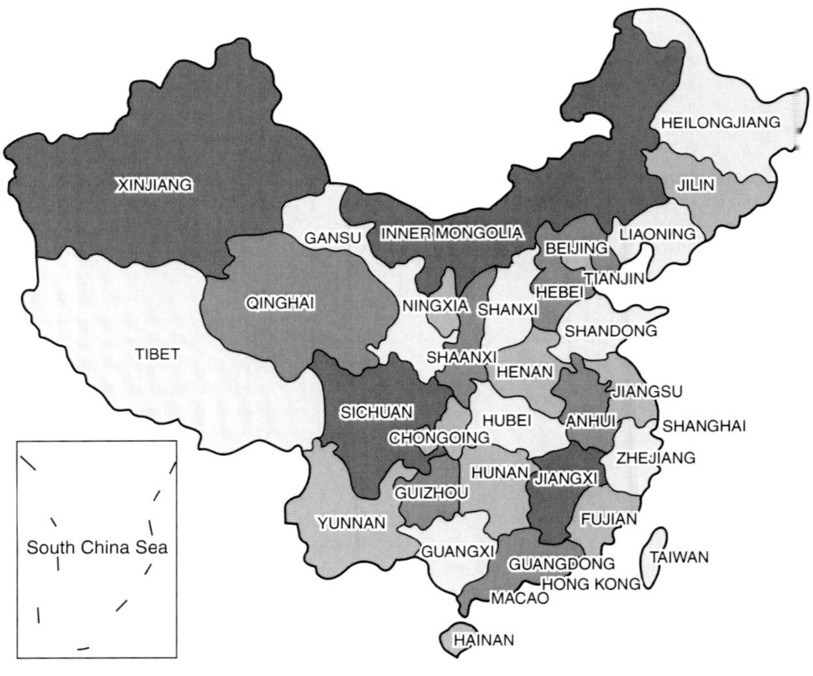

Figure 3.18 Map of China
Source: Gov.cn, 2006.

Table 3.14 presents China's trade with selected regions. The figures in the table show that Latin America and the Caribbean have been increasing its share of trade with China since 2000, the exports share have grown by 62% and the imports share by 166%. The Rest of the World has also increased its export and import share but only by 14% and 7% respectively. The EU has increased its exports share by 18.45% but the imports share has decreased by 7.43%. Asia Pacific and North America have both been decreasing their share in exports and imports.

Finally, the fact that China has become the world's second largest economy is only a part of this story. Beijing (北京), Shanghai (上海) and the provinces of Guangdong (广东省), Zhejiang (浙江), Jiangsu (江苏), Shandong (山东), Hebei (河北) and Henan (河南) have also been increasing their weight in the world's economy since the reforms started back in 1978. In fact, these six provinces 'are expected to have an annual GDP of over $1,000 billion within the next ten years. That puts them

Table 3.14 China's trade with Latin America and the Caribbean, Asia Pacific, North America, EU and rest of the world, in percentage

Exports	**2000**	**2001**	**2002**	**2003**	**2004**	**2005**	**2006**	**2007**	**2008**	**2009**
Latin America and the Caribbean	2.9	3.1	2.9	2.7	3.0	3.1	3.7	4.2	5	4.7
Asia Pacific	18.3	18.4	16.5	15.2	14.1	12.7	11.0	10.0	9.8	10.0
North America	22.2	21.7	22.8	22.4	22.5	23.0	22.7	20.7	19.2	19.9
EU	16.8	17	16.5	18.3	18.5	19.4	19.3	20.4	20.7	19.9
Rest of the World	39.8	39.8	41.3	41.4	41.9	41.8	43.3	44.7	45.3	45.5
Imports	**2000**	**2001**	**2002**	**2003**	**2004**	**2005**	**2006**	**2007**	**2008**	**2009**
Latin America and the Caribbean	2.4	2.7	2.8	3.6	3.9	4.0	4.3	5.3	6.3	6.4
Asia Pacific	21	20.1	20.4	20	19.1	17.9	17.2	16.9	16.8	17.2
North America	11.6	12.4	10.5	9.3	9.3	8.5	8.5	8.4	8.3	8.9
EU	14.8	15.9	14.4	14.1	13.4	11.9	12.1	12.4	12.5	13.7
Rest of the World	50.2	48.9	51.9	53	54.3	57.7	57.9	57	56.1	53.8

Source: UN, 2009a

above countries including Russia, Canada, and Spain' (Lall, 2010). In this context, for example Jiangsu, the largest recipient of foreign direct investments in the last four years and expected to overtake Guangdong as China's largest provincial economy, grew at the annual rate of 17% in 2010. On top of this, 'a further ten provinces – some of which are in the centre (for instance Sichuan -四川) and north (for instance Inner Mongolia -内蒙古) of China- will have GDPs between $500 billion and $1,000 billion by 2020, comparable to countries such as Indonesia, South Africa and Switzerland' (Lall, 2010). In other words, it seems that China will begin to resemble 'a collection of second-tier developed world and leading developing countries' (Zhiming, 2010, p. 10).

3.4 Conclusions

This chapter has presented evidence showing that China and Latin America's economies are getting closer. Flows of commerce (in both directions) and FDI (mainly from China, but increasingly from Latin America too) are growing at rates well above the figures seen in other regions, this axis of commerce was almost negligible ten years ago.

As seen, the two regions have completely different histories, they have grown within completely different cultural frameworks, and they have been under the influence of completely different political systems. However, and most importantly, they share many similarities and challenges. Both regions missed the opportunities brought by the Industrial Revolution and therefore started to increase their weight in the world's economy mainly in the last 20 years after a twentieth century full of political and economic changes. China and Latin America are among the largest producers of most commodities, being them low and/or intermediate technology manufactures or natural resources. Also both regions have big domestic markets in need of development, and also both have the challenge to make their internal markets less fragmented the UNASUR aims at having a single market by 2014 and the Chinese government is also working on reducing the internal barriers as 'access to foreign markets is easier and cheaper than access to most of the country's domestic markets' (Boisot and Meyer, 2008, p. 354).

Coincidentally, also the sizes of their main markets are similar. Table 3.14 presents selected economic and social indicators of the main Chinese provinces and Latin American countries. As can be seen, the population of the six largest Chinese provinces and two megacities is about 575 million and their combined economy measured in nominal GDP (2009) is US $3,472 billion. These figures compare to the nine

Table 3.15 Selected economic and social indicators for China, (main Chinese provinces) and Latin America (main Latin American countries)

	GDP (PPP) 2010	GDP (Nominal) 2009	GDP per capita (PPP) 2010	GDP per capita (Nominal) 2009	Population (mill)	Gini Index	Life exp. at birth	Literacy %
China	10084	4985	7517	3735	1336	41.5	74.68	91.6
Beijing	n/a	211	n/a	10602	70.3	n/a	n/a	n/a
Guangdong	n/a	696	n/a	6272	96.4	n/a	n/a	n/a
Hebei	n/a	309	n/a	3751	70.3	n/a	n/a	n/a
Henan	n/a	351	n/a	3144	94.9	n/a	n/a	n/a
Jiangsu	n/a	626	n/a	6829	77.2	n/a	n/a	n/a
Shandong	n/a	604	n/a	5480	94.7	n/a	n/a	n/a
Shanghai	n/a	258	n/a	11992	19.2	n/a	n/a	n/a
Zhejiang	n/a	417	n/a	6795	51.8	n/a	n/a	n/a
Latin America and the Caribbean	6354	3965	11188	n/a	590	n/a	n/a	n/a
Argentina	632	310	15603	7725	41.8	45.7	76.95	97.2
Brazil	2181	1574	11289	8220	203	56.7	72.53	88.6
Chile	257	161	14982	9515	16.9	52.4	77.7	95.7
Colombia	430	232	9445	5167	44.7	58.5	74.55	90.4
Costa Rica	51	29	10731	6345	4.6	48	77.72	94.9
Ecuador	114	56	7951	3935	15.1	46.9	75.73	91
Mexico	1549	875	14266	8134	113.7	48.2	76.47	86.1
Peru	274	127	9281	4356	29.2	49.6	72.47	92.9
Venezuela	347	326	11889	11383	27.6	41	73.93	93

Notes:
GDP (PPP) and GDP per capita (PPP) source IMF. GDP (PPP) expressed in billions of US dollars. GDP per capita (PPP) expressed in US dollars.
GDP and GDP per capita (Nominal) for China and Latin American countries source IMF, expressed in billions of US dollars.
GDP and GDP per capita (Nominal) for Chinese provinces source Deutsche Bank, transformed into US dollars from RMB (rate 1/0.1531).
Life expectancy at birth expressed in years source CIA.
Literacy expressed in per cent of people age 15 and over than can read and write; source CIA.
n/a: not available
Source: CIA, 2011c; Deutsche Bank, 2011b; IMF, 2010.

main Latin American countries with a population of around 497 million and a combined economy (also measured in nominal GDP in 2009) of US $3,690 billion.

In addition, comparing the figures from Table 3.15 and similar to the case of China, it can also be said that Latin America seems to be a collection of second-tier developed world and leading developing countries. This idea supports the existence of opportunities for mutual gains, and also that companies from the two regions can continue benefiting from the strengthening of this commercial relationship. This is particularly important as (1) Latin American companies can sell in China commodities (where they have comparative and competitive advantages) that are not allowed to compete freely, for example in the EU due to the Common Agricultural Policy (CAP)[17] or in the United States due to the agricultural subsidies, (2) Chinese companies can find in Latin America a growing middle class for their low and intermediate technology manufactures, and (3) the export baskets of both regions are complementary. This also shows that allowing access to markets to emerging economies can help them in their economic development process.

Finally, the data presented in this chapter support two of the ideas presented in Chapter 2. First, cities are the real emerging markets (see Section 2.6), the 17 countries/provinces included in Table 3.15 are dominated by a big city (or two as the case of Brazil) usually with more than 10 million inhabitants (see Table 2.7). Second, the commercial relationship between China and Latin America is establishing itself as the emerging markets' axis (Fornes, 2011). This is the first strong axis between emerging economies, and it is highly likely that new strong axes of trade and investments will start to appear in the near future especially when countries like India increases their presence in international trade (see Table 2.3) as companies will start to exploit the opportunities offered by a China–India axis, or by a Latin America–India axis.

4
Rivals and Partners?

> Though China and Latin America and the Caribbean are far from each other, the two peoples enjoy a time-honoured friendship. The two sides are at a similar stage of development.... To enhance solidarity and cooperation with other developing countries is the cornerstone of China's independent foreign policy of peace. The Chinese government views its relations with Latin America and the Caribbean from a strategic plane and seeks to build and develop a comprehensive and cooperative partnership featuring equality, mutual benefit and common development with Latin American and Caribbean countries.
>
> Extracts from sections II and III of China's Policy Paper on Latin America and the Caribbean (2008) – printed in full as Appendix 1.

> If every Chinese person eats a banana from Ecuador each day, then our foreign relations problems will be solved.
>
> President Gustavo Noboa of Ecuador at the start of a state visit to China, March 2002 (Agence France Presse, 2009)

4.1 Introduction

Western societies, their leaders and opinion formers still have difficulty coming to terms with China's extraordinary and rapid rise as a global power. Their lack of familiarity with China's centralised and Communist-led political and economic system is one reason for this.

China's huge geographical size and its 1.3 billion people are other reasons. The speed of China's economic growth, reaching on occasion a growth rate of 10% per annum or more, is a further source of wonderment and curiosity that separates China from the known experience and understanding of most people in the West. China's economic transition and transformation since the 1980s is impressive by any standard. Any parallel transition from a political and social perspective is more opaque, and is much less easy to measure or to assess.

4.2 What is China seeking from its engagement with Latin America?

The first concerns of Chinese MNEs in looking to trade with and invest in Latin America have been to secure access to mineral and energy resources to supply the manufacturing base of their home economy, as well as food supplies (notably soya) with which to feed the country's large population. But China's involvement with Latin America goes considerably beyond this. China is also interested in selling its largely manufactured goods to the emerging markets of Latin America, a classic example of the long advocated, but until now little practised, South–South trade first called for by the Brandt Report in the early 1980s (Independent Commission on International Development Issues and Brandt, 1980). A major landmark facilitating this process was China's becoming a member of the World Trade Organisation in 2001. China now has two free trade agreements in place in the region – with Chile since 2004 (see Appendix 4) and with Peru since 2007 (Appendix 5) – as evidence of a broadening and maturing economic partnership between states. A further free trade agreement with Costa Rica was signed in April 2010 although its ratification had not been completed in early 2011 (Appendix 6).

The scope of this kind of economic partnership would appear to extend beyond the obvious targets of trade and foreign direct investment to include infrastructure, which may assist the efficient transfer of goods (mainly road links to the major ports, given the abandonment of Latin America's railways in the second half of the twentieth century) and the efficient conduct of business (e.g., telecommunications). The most ambitious infrastructure so far that the Chinese are financing is the plan to provide an alternative to the Panama Canal by building a direct rail link between ports on Colombia's Atlantic and Pacific coasts (see Section 3.2.). The longer the Chinese stay in Latin America, and few would doubt that this is the start of a long-term relationship, the more the Chinese are likely to involve themselves in other aspects of the local economies of their host countries. Already it has been noticed how the Chinese presence is beginning to marginalise the much longer established Japanese economic ties, for example in Mexico and in Peru. If Chinese engagement with Latin America is driven by necessity and opportunism, then there should be no inherent barrier to Chinese investment in non-extractive industry targets, not least to supply goods and services to the small but growing Chinese expatriate communities in various Latin American states, but also to acquire, and so to take advantage of technological innovation as it arises.

In addition, the long-term involvement of China in Central and South American states indicates that a similar approach is being adopted to what analysts and academic observers have found to be underpinning China's new ties to Africa. China seems willing to invest in almost all states whatever their political system or relative political stability, provided business can be done and investments made to pay. Here China's current doctrine of the 'Four No's' (no hegemonism, no power politics, no arms races and no military alliances) comes into play with potential advantage (see Section 3.2). China is a nonjudgmental global economic actor, willing to invest where others fear to tread. Western analysts have sometimes suggested that such a nonjudgmental approach to political regimes (e.g., side-stepping the continuing power play in Zimbabwe or continuing support for Equatorial Guinea) is borne of necessity. Western MNEs may well have cornered the sources of supply for energy and mineral resources in more reliable and capitalist-friendly states, but Chinese companies have also earned a friendlier welcome in some of the riskier resource-rich states and, in Latin America, have adopted more prudent and slower entry strategies than, for example, French and Spanish MNCs that splashed out on high profile, and often unremunerative investments in the 1990s (Fornes, 2009).

The low profile approach preferred by China and Chinese MNEs has not prevented the Chinese government on occasion from making decisive interventions on a broader economic front. A recent example is the decision of the Chinese authorities to offer a $1 billion loan to the Ecuadorian government to finance a significant programme of investment in infrastructure, construction and telecommunications (see Section 3.2.). A similar arrangement with the United States or a European state such as Spain might well have attracted criticism, and perhaps could have been seen as evidence of superpower hegemony or post-colonial dependency. The Chinese government does not carry such political baggage and, as the world's largest holder of foreign exchange reserves (estimated to be in excess of US $3 trillion in value) it is increasingly well placed to offer economic and financial support to Latin American and other governments across the world if it so wishes.

So far there is plenty of evidence to suggest that China's strategy in regard to Latin America is to develop focused bilateral relations with individual states in order to facilitate investment and trade, as has already been observed in Africa (Alden and Hughes, 2009). Chinese interests may have initiated foreign direct investment in Latin America for the purpose of resource-seeking and asset-exploitation, but there is now some evidence that Chinese interests are also acquiring strategic assets for market-seeking purposes – partly as a result of the saturation of parts of the Chinese market (Fornes and Butt-Philip, 2011a).

However, such market-seeking strategies may lead in turn to Chinese exports threatening the survival of Latin American domestic producers. The expansion of trade can be in both directions, of course, and China still needs to find markets for its ever-growing output of manufactured goods. China can also offer political support for individual states seeking membership of important international organisations such as APEC. But bilateral relations of this nature, with a succession of different states from the same continent, open the way for conflicts of interest to emerge. The more bilateral relations are developed, the greater the need for the two sides of the relationship to develop a strong mutual understanding on which profitable and sustainable continuing engagement can be based. Table 4.1 highlights the differing portfolio of Latin American exports to China, country by country, and the similarity of their imports.

The big surprise of the 1990s for Latin America proved to be the replacement of US companies by firms from the EU, especially Spain, but also France, as the principal foreign direct investors in their continent (Fornes, 2009). Many of these investments proved to be problematic, and in the following decade, foreign direct investors form the EU ceded poll position in Latin America to Chinese enterprises (Fornes, 2009; Fornes and Butt-Philip, 2011a). In part, tougher trading conditions in their domestic markets, and then the seismic impacts of the financial and economic crises since 2007 will have led to an across the board reduction of FDI, if not actual withdrawal from Latin American markets, as far as American and European MNEs were concerned. Chinese MNEs were much less troubled by such issues and the annual growth rate experienced by the Chinese economy did not drop below 7% after the year 2000. Such a difference of trading experiences, domestic business environments and commercial outcomes in terms of cash flow,

Table 4.1 Trade relations between China and Latin American states

	China buys	**China sells**
China/Mexico	Oil, soya, manufactures	Manufactures, textiles
China/Peru	Minerals, fish products	Manufactures, textiles
China/Chile	Copper	Manufactues, textiles
China/Argentina	Oil, soya, meat	Manufactures, textiles
China/Brazil	Aircraft, oil, soya	Manufactures, components, textiles
China/Venezuela	Oil	Manufactures, textiles
China/Ecuador	Bananas, oil, fish powder	Manufactures, textiles, construction equipment

Source: ECLAC, 2010b.

and ultimately funds available for investment, has inevitably reinforced the leading role played by China and Chinese interests as foreign direct investors in Latin America. This dominance continues and appears to be gathering momentum.

On paper, almost all Chinese foreign direct investment into the region would seem to be headed for the two global tax havens of the British Virgin Islands and the Cayman Islands. We have argued in Chapter 3 that these are not the final destinations of such investment funds, but tax efficient staging posts. The funds do not even stay in the Caribbean, but instead get moved to locations in central and southern America. Moreover there were still three Central American or Caribbean states in 2009 (Honduras, the Dominican Republic and Belize) with no recorded Chinese foreign direct investment at all (see Table 3.6).

The Chinese MNEs investing in Latin America do so for largely instrumental commercial reasons, and not at the behest of the Chinese government. Just as in Africa, their major concern is to secure access to resources vital to keep their operations in China fully functioning and their population fed. Their investments are much more a reflection of their perceived vulnerability than any attempt to ratchet up China's economic power, let alone to realise any imperial ambitions or play power games with other major global actors (Jiang, 2009). Chinese investments are first and foremost designed to ensure long-term access to strategic resources which will preserve, if not strengthen, China's place as the world's leading manufacturing country. At the same time Chinese approaches to their own enterprise's corporate governance suggest that they will expect the state (as at home) to be responsible for managing any societal and/or economic concerns from the activities arising from the resource extraction process, such as in mining, quarrying refining and transport (Haglund, 2009).

If there are political risks stemming from the eclectic selection of economic partner states by Chinese MNEs, whether or not their political regimes are stable, democratic or respectable in the eyes of world opinion, there may also be advantages in having investments in a large portfolio of such partner states on the assumption that political and economic risks sufficient to disrupt trade are unlikely to occur in many of them at the same time. There may, however, be local political issues in which their neutrality and the distancing of Chinese interests from the government at all levels could become a problem. There is not usually much contact or engagement with local communities by Chinese investors. Their managers in the field are typically on short-term contracts and so the chance for them to become well dug in locally is rare. This practice of manager rotation may even discourage longer term strategic planning on the ground (Large, 2009). If local political problems threaten their own expatriates some quiet intervention may occur, as happened in Africa in the Sudan where the Chinese government was able discreetly to encourage a de-escalation of civil war hostilities (Large, 2009).

But otherwise, Chinese MNEs do not face domestic pressures at home in China from human rights or pro-democracy constituencies, so it is relatively easy for China and its enterprises to offer financial aid economic cooperation, investment and sometimes even international political support to autocratic regimes (Esteban, 2009). People in China as well as the government, are likely to approach their involvement in the development of Latin American economies – much as they have in regard to Africa – as an occasion for solidarity and the realisation of opportunities for both sides, and not simply as the development of locations for assuring the security of supply of critical energy, mineral and food products.

But the best outcomes are likely to be achieved when there is a good local working relationship between Chinese investors and local government, and including local communities too, so that a real sense of ownership and partnership between stakeholders is allowed to develop, enabling capacity-building issues that emerge (such as over education and training, or in regard to local infrastructure improvement) to be addressed constructively.

4.3 What is Latin America seeking from its engagement with China?

There are dangers in trying to generalise about the aspirations of Latin America because of the great diversity of resources, social institutions and levels of economic development that distinguish its various nation states one from another. In population terms, the two states of Brazil (196 million) and Mexico (110 million) overshadow all the others, and their independent presence as world traders is already significant – Mexico being the world's tenth largest exporter and importer, while Brazil is the world's eighteenth largest exporter and importer (see **Table 2.3**). China has become a very important market for six Latin American countries – Brazil, Chile and Peru above all, with Argentina, Cuba and Costa Rica also in this frame. Several countries in this region remain relatively untouched by China's interest in foreign direct investment in Latin America, yet they are still affected by China's growing profile and position in world trade (Jenkins, 2008). A country as cut off from the economic mainstream as Paraguay still finds that China is the lead provider of its imports (Jenkins, 2008).

Trade between China and Latin America overall has, however, multiplied more than tenfold since the year 2000 – and Brazil's largest trading partner is now China. The same is also true for Chile. The profile of goods exported by Latin American states to China is varied. More developed economies such as Brazil are exporting Embraer aircraft to China while Mexico exports car components. But the main products sent to China from Latin America are from the food, minerals and energy sectors – soya, edible oils, coffee, copper, lithium, oil and gas. The spectacular growth of China's economy has created a higher than ever demand for such products, and of course it has also greatly contributed to the simultaneous rise in hard and soft commodity prices worldwide. While this phenomenon has greatly benefitted most Latin American economies in terms of increased activity and revenues from exports, there is an important downside as well. Latin American states are wary of economic success that is so closely tied to a boom in commodity prices whose tendency to oscillate between boom and bust is well known. Even so developed an economy as Mexico is apprehensive that the pressure to supply such primary products in greater quantities than ever may postpone or even put in jeopardy the country's long-term strategy to stimulate and to expand its manufacturing base. Prioritising the latter objective is intended to help create a more balanced economy and an economy with more reliable prospects for economic growth in the medium and longer term based on adding value through manufacturing operations and processes (Private interview with Mexican official).

The growth of China's economy makes that model of development more difficult to realise, not only because of the boom in demand for fuels, commodities and food but, more worryingly, because the success of China's development in manufacturing challenges the very competitiveness of an economy, such as that of Mexico or Brazil, when they are making and selling similar goods worldwide – such as textiles (Blazquez-Lidoy et al., 2006). For these economies to become more reliant upon the export of food, fuels and other commodities, while less able to export more sophisticated manufactured goods would represent a major step backwards in terms of their future development. This is a particularly grave concern for Mexico – more than most other states. These indirect effects of China's growing global economic presence have become the subjects of several influential studies by academics and policy makers (Blazquez-Lidoy et al., 2006; Jenkins, Dussel Peters, and Moreira, 2008).

Box 4.1 China in talks with Brazil over trade barriers (Pearson, 2011a)

China is in talks with Brazil on lifting trade barriers that would allow the Latin American country to sell it more processed agricultural goods, Brazilian government officials have told the *Financial Times*.

During the negotiations in Brasilia last week with Chen Deming, China's commerce minister, Brazil's government gave Beijing a list of ten processed goods it wants to start exporting in quantity, such as frozen chicken wings and soybean oil.

The move is the first stage in a plan to sell more value-added goods to Asia.

'The relationship with China is so unbalanced, not only in terms of value but in terms of what we trade', one official close to the trade negotiations said. 'The Chinese acknowledge this and said they will make an effort to change this.'

Iron ore, soybeans and petroleum account for about 80% of Brazil's exports to China, partly because more heavily processed goods are restricted by higher tariffs. Brazil claims tariffs on soybean oil are nine times higher than the charge on raw soybeans. Meanwhile, China mainly sends back cheap manufactured components such as television and air conditioning parts.

Economists have warned that if Brazil cannot soon start exporting more processed goods, it is in danger of falling victim to 'Dutch disease', whereby commodity-driven currency appreciation crushes local manufacturing.

Speaking to reporters last Monday, Mr Chen said that China welcomed more diversified exports from Brazil. 'We hope that good Brazilian products can be introduced into the Chinese market,' he said, adding that it was ultimately up to the Chinese consumer to decide.

Brazil also called on China to promote the sale of Brazilian luxury shoes and jewellery in its domestic market. 'We cannot compete with China on prices; that's not the point,' the Brazilian official said, adding that the government believed it could challenge countries such as Italy in China's luxury shoe shops. Brazil's new president, Dilma Rousseff, last month made one of her first overseas trips to China in a bid to diversify trade.

As the Brazilian currency has soared almost 50% against the dollar since the end of 2008, putting pressure on local manufacturers, Brazil's government has also taken more measures to slow various imports.

Earlier this month, Brazil said it would delay granting licences to imported vehicles in an attempt to reduce the number of cars coming from abroad, causing outrage in Argentina, the biggest vehicle exporter to the country.

Brazil is looking at introducing similar measures on other products, the government official said, as the country tries to buy itself time while it evaluated the problems facing individual sectors.

Brasilia has launched anti-dumping investigations and imposed limits on imports of some Chinese goods to protect domestic industry but officials will be wary of imposing too many trade restrictions out of fear of retaliation from China.

In neighbouring Argentina, new tariffs introduced last year on cheap Chinese imports in order to protect local industry were met by retaliatory action from Beijing, which effectively banned imports of soybean products from Argentina in response.

It is also clear that the export performance of Latin America in recent years has been much weaker than that of China (Blazquez-Lidoy et al., 2006; Jenkins et al., 2008). Some Latin American states can show a solid export growth trajectory since the year 2000 as far as exports to China are concerned – Chile, Brazil, Peru and Costa Rica stand out. There are, however, many Latin American states showing very little change in the share of their exports that are going to China, the most significant of which is Mexico. The same desultory export performance is true also for the states of the Caribbean. There is even some evidence to suggest that Chinese MNEs are able to out-compete Latin American firms in Latin American markets (Jenkins et al., 2008).

Mexico is responding to the Chinese challenge by seeking to leverage its position as a member of NAFTA with immediate access to the American market. It is seeking to offer tax free enterprise zones, as well as swift, cheap port, transit and customs clearance facilities in order to compete with more direct channels for trade with North America. A striking example of this is to be found in San Luis Potosi, once a silver mining centre and now an industrial city specialising in car manufacturing, where several road and rail networks converge. Other cities such as the port of Colima on the Pacific coast are seeking to adopt the San Luis Potosi model (Private interview with San Luis Potosi official).

Nevertheless, at the everyday level the increased interest on the part of China in trading with and investing in Latin American economies is welcomed across the continent. The government of the People's Republic of China has clearly indicated, most recently in a policy paper of 2008, that it is actively seeking an expanded trading and investment relationship with Latin America (see Appendix 1). There have been numerous bilateral visits in both directions at ministerial and official level in recent years (see Table 3.1). Despite the friendly and favourable political rhetoric it would also be a mistake to infer that Chinese interests are approaching Latin American governments with an open cheque book. One Latin American president commented in 2009 that negotiating with the government of China was worse than negotiating with the International Monetary Fund (Agence France Presse, 2009). It would be equally erroneous to infer from all this activity that all Chinese economic activity in Central and Southern America is centrally directed by either the government or the Communist party in Beijing. There are far too many links in play for such a scenario to be realistic (Private interviews with Mexican officials). The framework for Chinese trade and investment has been set out by the government of China, most clearly in the 2008 policy paper (see Appendix 1), but the implementation of this policy is left very much in the hands of Chinese enterprises. The relations that Latin American authorities are developing on the ground are with the Chinese MNEs, more than the Chinese government.

The recession and the economic stagnation in North America and Western Europe since 2008 have increased the relative economic importance of China, whose economic growth and development has continued to surge. Politically most regimes in Latin America are preoccupied with tackling poverty, marshalling all the resources they can command to foster development, combating inflation, while limiting the power of criminal gangs, drug cartels, terrorists and other anti-government elements. Chinese trade and investment helps to keep the politics and the economics of the continent stable.

Historically, North American and European MNCs have found Latin America to be a much more attractive location than China – for reasons of proximity; of language, culture and society; as well as the level of development – at least in some parts. The total FDI stock held by North American and European interests in Latin America was more than two and a half times the size (by value) of the FDI stock they had amassed in the People's Republic of China (see Table 2.4).

Latin America has for centuries been dependent for its development upon external investment. Now it finds itself competing with China to be the investment location of choice for firms from developed countries, such as the EU and the United States. The evidence in Chapter 3 suggests that even now Latin America is significantly more attractive to foreign investors than the PRC and that net foreign direct investment has been rising faster in Latin America than in the PRC in the period 2000–2009 (up 210% in Latin America compared with a rise of 145% in the PRC over the same period). A large part of this new foreign direct investment in Latin America has in fact come from the People's Republic of China, but this still represents a small fraction of the total FDI stock invested in Latin America, although bigger investment projects backed by China are now under way (see Section 3.2.).

If there is a potential conflict of interest between Chinese investments and their host regimes in Latin America this could arise in regard to the natural environment in the face of new development. Much of China's investment in the region so far is directed to mining and quarrying for mineral extraction, as well as towards building or improving the infrastructure. Given that Chinese enterprises, as noted earlier, expect restrictions on environmental damage arising from their operations to be regulated by government authorities in each locality, rather than be left as a matter for self-regulation, this opens up some potential for conflict with local community interests which place more importance on protecting their local environment (and sometimes as well the traditional patterns of subsistence and occupation) than on economic development and new job creation. The typically rather tenuous links between Chinese MNEs and civil society, wherever in the world they operate, may thus leave these MNEs, and their local managers in particular, rather exposed to criticism and controversy. In the short term such concerns are unlikely to prove much of an obstacle to developments in Latin America, which are led by Chinese investors. The very different governments across the region's many nation states are likely to give precedence to the need to meet rising economic expectations of their rapidly growing populations. Chinese interest in growing its trade and investment portfolio with so many Latin American states is the next best thing to manna from heaven.

More forward-looking authorities and investors may also come to understand that Latin America does not always have to compete directly with China to earn its keep. A clear pointer for future investment is the development of the tourist industry, as indicated in Chapter 3. Major infrastructure investment as well as the expansion of tourist services across the region ought to be able to take advantage of much of the great expansion of tourism by Chinese nationals expected in the next decade. Nor is this just an opportunity for Chinese investors, but for local private and public investment initiatives, as well as for investors from North America and Europe. The attraction of Latin America for Chinese people is likely in part to follow from the shared development goals and mutual understanding so clearly indentified in the 2008 Chinese government Policy Paper (see Appendix 1), as for more conventional reasons such as visiting historic heritage sites and experiencing natural phenomena.

4.4 Conclusions

China has adopted a nonjudgmental political approach to Latin America since its primary interest in trade and investment there is economic, and above all resource-seeking. There are signs that China's reach is spreading into other parts of Latin American economies as its own domestic markets become saturated and the development of Latin American economies provides excellent opportunities for trade. However, not all of the economies in Latin America and the Caribbean are benefitting from China's interest to the same extent.

China's official rhetoric revolves around the core message that China is one developing country that is now in a position to help others develop similarly without being encumbered by the historical baggage of colonialism. Problems may arise if and when the resources that China is seeking to exploit form part of an environment that local populations in Latin America wish to preserve.

Latin America welcomes Chinese trade and investment, but with some misgivings, as a mixed blessing. Chinese exports to Latin America pose a clear competitive threat to domestic producers, while China's purchases from Latin America (mainly minerals, food and energy) risk locking Latin American states into an unbalanced economic model in which there is little manufacturing output and in which their economies are at the mercy of volatile commodity prices. Latin America has few alternative strategies to choose from in the short term. In the long run regional economic integration ought to be able to make a significant contribution to each state's economic development. In the current climate China's big pitch into Latin America risks slowing down the existing momentum for regional economic integration.

5

Chinese Dragons Disembarking in Latin America

> The capabilities to succeed in emerging markets will be decisive in the next round of global competition.[1]

5.1 Introduction[2]

Since the start of the reforms by Deng Xiaoping in 1978 the world's economy has witnessed two major changes about China. The first change was the opening of the economy to foreign capital, which made China one of the largest recipients of foreign direct investment in the twenty-first century and transformed the country in what is now known as 'the factory of the world'. The second change was the international expansion of Chinese companies first into developed economies and then also into emerging markets, which is transforming China's firms (dubbed the Chinese Dragons by many commentators) into global players.

This international expansion started to attract the attention from the media and specialised publications mainly when Leonovo acquired the former IBM PC Company Division in 2005 for approximately US $1.75 billion. Other international acquisitions of well known brands by Chinese firms were made public at that time, like Nanjing Automobile's acquisition of MG Rover in the UK, or TCL's joint venture (called TTE, TCL and Thomson Electronics) with Thomson from France to manufacture RCA and Thomson TV and DVD products. This first wave of acquisitions was followed by a string of initial public offerings (IPOs) from Chinese State-owned enterprises (SOE) that also attracted the attention from almost everyone in business. In October 2006 the flotation in Hong Kong and Shanghai of the Industrial and Commercial Bank of China (ICBC) was one of the first of these IPOs, raising US $21.9 billion for a 17% stake. It is the world's largest ever IPO (attracting more than US $500 billion in orders worldwide and eclipsing the $18.4 billion flotation of NTT DoCoMo from Japan in 1998) (McGregor, Mitchell, and Dyer, 2006). Nowadays, news of Chinese companies visiting different countries on a shopping spree is found in almost every newspaper and magazine. This international expansion of Chinese companies is the focus of this chapter as they are the main players operating in Latin America.

5.2 Chinese companies' main characteristics

When analysing Chinese companies it is important to consider that many of China's international firms remain in state hands. Although most of them have been corporatised, this means that most 'firms still align their operations, whether at home or abroad, with the five-year plans and national imperatives' (Buckley, Clegg, Cross, Liu, Voss, and Zheng, 2007). This is mainly because, in spite of the reforms, the Communist Party of China still maintains 'full control of the country's affairs and keeps firmly committed to many of socialism's key tenets'. 'Indeed, the state – and the Party – are central players in nearly all aspects of China's economy, guiding a development trajectory often labelled as capitalism with social characteristics' (Spar and Oi, 2006, p. 1).

It is in this context that China's economy started its outward internationalisation process at the end of the 1970s as a result of the government-led open-door policy (Cai, 1999; Tseng, 1994). In this process it is possible to identify three main stages: a first stage mainly 'experimental' up to the 1990s that was characterised by strong supervision from the government; a second stage during the 1990s with a large increase in the number of Chinese subsidiaries abroad but with little strategic focus and with many of them reporting losses (Cai, 1999; Quan, 2004; Warner, Ng, and Xu, 2004; Zhang and Van Den Bulcke, 1996); and finally, a third stage that started with China's accession to the WTO in 2001 and that is seeing many leading Chinese firms going international with the clear intention to become global players in international markets (Child and Rodrigues, 2005).

Chinese companies have been taking three main routes towards their internationalisation (Child and Rodrigues, 2005). The first route has been partnering with international companies through original equipment manufacture (OEM) or joint venture (JV) agreements. Although this route has usually been regarded as inward internationalisation, in the case of China it has acted as a way to transfer knowledge from the international partner and as a consequence improving Chinese firms' competitiveness. The second route has been M&As, a route supported by an international shopping spree in different countries and also in different industries. The third route has been the establishment of greenfield subsidiaries and facilities in targeted markets. See Table 3.6, Table 3.7, and Table 3.8 for figures on China's outward foreign direct investment.

This internationalisation process has been supported by a set of drivers and facilitators (Child and Rodrigues, 2005, p. 399). Among the drivers the following can be mentioned:

Hazard of relying on a highly competitive domestic market with low margins;
Opportunities to export based on domestic cost advantages;
Potential to complement domestic cost advantages with differentiation advantages acquired abroad;
The need to secure and develop advanced technology and internationally recognized brands; and
The desire to gain entrepreneurial and managerial freedom.

The identified facilitators are:

strong governmental support for globalization, especially financial backing and tolerance of domestic moves (such as M&A) that build corporate strength;
ability to reach a favorable accommodation with government, so as to combine support with strategic freedom to act entrepreneurially, raise capital abroad, etc.;
access to state-supported scientific and technical research; and
The willingness of foreign firms to sell or share international-standard technology, know-how, and brands.

The internationalisation stages mentioned above were accompanied also by developments in the capabilities in Chinese firms. At the time of the first two stages most studies suggested (1) that Chinese international firms tended to rely on their diaspora for business abroad, (2) that the local and central governments had a big influence on outward foreign investments, and (3) that the capabilities of China's international firms were relatively weak in comparison with their Western counterparts.

For (1) it was seen that Chinese firms operating overseas tended to lean on ethnic and other similar networks for business opportunities, relations with local authorities and management of labour (Brown, 1995; Lecraw, 1993; Yeung and Olds, 2000). For example, it was found that 'ethnic Chinese networks have a quantitatively important impact on bilateral trade through mechanisms of market information and matching and referral services, in addition to their effect through community enforcement of sanctions that deter opportunistic behaviour' (Rauch and Trindade, 2002, p. 129), and that Chinese managers use these networks as a way of reducing transaction costs and exploring new business opportunities (Boisot and Child, 1996).

For (2), it was observed that the central and local governments encouraged and directed many of the outward FDI processes with the aim of promoting exports and securing raw materials, although some state-owned companies also used their investments abroad to acquire technology and skills (Cai, 1999; Child and Rodrigues, 2005).

For (3) it was seen that the competitive capabilities of both state-owned and non-state enterprises were relatively weak in comparison with their Western counterparts mainly in the areas of R&D, marketing ability, development of brands, etc. Probably this was the result of the government's protection of the domestic market, advantageous funding conditions, distribution channels protections and procurement from the government (Nolan, 2001). In fact, after the first wave of international acquisitions by Chinese MNEs it was suggested that these operations mainly reflected 'China's country-specific advantages (CSAs) rather than FSAs' (firm-specific advantages) (Rugman and Li, 2007, p. 71).

Since the beginnings of the third stage of internationalisation different views have appeared discussing the pillars in which Chinese international companies base their internationalisation process. This has even started a debate in the specialised academic literature (see Box 3.4) One of the first to provide a different approach to analyse Chinese international companies were Zeng and Williamson (2003) who claimed to have found a 'new breed of Chinese companies that have already succeeded in capturing some foreign markets'. These firms can be grouped in: (1) national champions, companies using their domestic strength to compete abroad, (2) dedicated exporters, enterprises aiming at acquiring market share in international markets to strengthen their economies of scale, (3) competitive networks, groups of companies that 'have taken on world markets by bringing together small, specialized companies that operate in close proximity', and (4) technology up-starts, firms exploiting technology developed by research institutes owned by the government (pp. 3–4).

Box 5.1 Chinese international companies in the academic literature (Fornes and Butt-Philip, 2011b, pp. 101–103)

The main question seems to be 'whether FDI from emerging economies and, specifically, from China requires a special theory nested within the general theory' (Buckley et al., 2007). Most of the literature on the internationalisation of companies from emerging countries is based on mainstream theory developed in Western economies from their multinational corporations adapted to the specific characteristics of developing countries, for example Lecraw (1993) and Wells (1983). However, in the case of China it has been suggested that an extended theoretical framework may be applied due to its newly developed capitalist system, its culture, and its different market institutions (Boisot and Child, 1996; Child and Rodrigues, 2005; Child and Tse, 2001). After all, 'China is different from other less developed countries in terms of market size as well as cultural connections and may not fall into a regular LDC category' (Makino et al., 2002, p. 412) and 'is already a much more open economy than most emerging markets' (Blazquez-Lidoy et al., 2006). Santiso (2005a, 2005b) also suggested that Chinese internationalisation has presented a particular 'cognitive effect' as it has been very pragmatic and the result of balanced efforts between markets and government intervention.

In this context, Child and Rodrigues (2005, pp. 384–385) claimed that the specific characteristics of the Chinese outward internationalisation process need to be analysed on their own merits. The first point supporting their claim is that China's emergence as an industrial power falls within the late development thesis (also applied to other East Asian countries) as China's companies need to catch up in terms of technology, know-how, and in the development of competitive business environments. Their argument in this area is based on Chinese firms' need to use outward FDI to close the gap with Western MNEs through the acquisition of assets and resources rather than by the exploitation of prior competitive advantages, the main assumption in mainstream theory (Buckley and Casson, 1976; Dunning, 1977).

Their second point concerns the Chinese government's role in its companies' internationalisation process as many firms have received financial support and protection from the authorities to reduce their late-coming disadvantage.

The third point is the counterpart of the second: the companies receiving support and aid as described 'could be weakened by the way they remain beholden to administrative approval and bear a legacy of institutional dependence' which may suggest that their strategic options are limited from the Chinese institutionalised environment.

The fourth point supporting their claim concerns Chinese culture and institutions (including, for example, the reliance on close personal relationships or their management styles) which may increase their psychic distance (Johanson and Wiedersheim-Paul, 1975). This liability of foreignness could eventually put the effectiveness of the strategy of acquiring resources abroad in jeopardy.

Mathews (2006) also added three more characteristics: very rapid internationalisation, internationalisation achieved through organisational innovations (rather than based on technological innovations) and the development of strategic innovations that enabled 'them to exploit their latecomer and peripheral status to advantage' (p. 13).

Based on these characteristics, Mathews proposed an extension of the OLI paradigm (Dunning, 1977) as this traditional model uses 'a 'push-oriented' concept' from Western MNEs where the firm's internationalisation 'is propelled by some strategic objective', rather than by a pull and push process that seems to be the reality for most Asian Pacific companies (Mathews, 2006, p. 16). This extended model, LLL (Linkage, Leveraging and Learning), is also supported by the idea that the internationalisation of 'EE [emerging markets]-based firms is not necessarily based on the possession of overwhelming assets, but rather on a firm's ability to leverage its capability in organizational learning' (Yamakawa, Peng, and Deeds, 2008, p. 68).

Nevertheless, these views are contrasted with previous findings from Cai (1999) who suggested that 'the motives for Chinese outward FDI are generally similar to those for FDI from other developing and developed market economies', even if the links with the authorities are visible. In this sense, Cai listed the following motives for outward FDI: (1) 'to seek, maintain or expand export markets', (2) 'to acquire a stable supply of resources', (3) 'to obtain foreign technology and management skills', (4) 'to raise capital, primarily in Hong Kong, for domestic use', and (5) for 'political considerations' (pp. 867–874). Wong and Chan (2003) added to this list (6) saturation in the home market, and (7) avoidance of non-tariff barriers. In addition, Wong and Chan (2003) and Cai (1999) agreed that 'China lacks personnel who possess international management skills and who have sufficient knowledge about market conditions of host countries...and a good understanding of the intricacies of international [business,] largely as a result of its long-time isolation from the world economy' (Cai, 1999, p. 874).

Finally, in one of the first works modelling Chinese outward direct investments (ODI), Buckley et al. (2007) found that, on the one hand, the determinants of these ODI are market size, natural resource endowments, institutional environment, policy liberalisation/home country institutions and cultural proximity. On the other hand, they also found that 'Chinese ODI is attracted, rather than deterred, by political risk', that China's capital market imperfections play an important role (especially in the measurement of risks), that state ownership can be considered as a firm-specific advantage and that these factors combined 'may have equipped Chinese MNEs with the special ownership advantages needed to be competitive in other emerging economies'. They concluded by arguing that 'for the present, Chinese outward investors clearly present marked contrasts from the conventional model in key aspects'; in other words, these investments have 'both a conventional and an idiosyncratic dimension' (pp 513–514).

In line with this, recent studies seem to support the idea that Chinese international companies have evolved from their two first stages of internationalisation. Big international firms from China rely less on their diaspora and they are increasingly recruiting graduates from top Western and Chinese universities. This change is probably due to the fact that the companies currently going abroad are different from the family businesses that left China 20 to 30 years ago. In this sense, the Chinese that have been leaving abroad for more than a decade or two do not necessarily have the training, knowledge and/or capabilities to work in big business (Fornes and Butt-Philip, 2011a).

The role and format of the support from the government also seem to be changing. For example, 'as a private enterprise, Galanz [the world's largest producer of microwave ovens] still finds it difficult to obtain loans from state-owned banks' (Ge and Ding, 2008, p.680). Also, studies on Chinese SMEs (Cardoza and Fornes, 2009; Fornes and Cardoza, 2010; Li, Fornes, and Cardoza, 20010; Xu, Fornes, and Cardoza, 2009; Xu, Fornes, and Cardoza, 2010) found that the support from the state in the form of funding seems to be instrumental only in the first stages (local and regional) of Chinese SMEs' international expansion and that ownership by the state does not seem to play a role in their internationalisation process. This appears to be a consequence of the number of companies currently crossing China's frontiers; it would be almost impossible to help all of them.

In terms of competitive capabilities, it has also been claimed that 'it is incorrect to see the pursuit of global aspirations by Chinese companies simply as a game of 'catch-up' with established multinationals' (Williamson and Yin, 2009, p. 98) as the Chinese dragons seem to have developed a set of distinctive capabilities that positioned them well to compete in a global environment. According to Williamson and Yin (2009, pp. 81–87) these distinctive capabilities of Chinese companies are:

- Cost innovation capabilities: the possibility of using China's cost advantage in new ways to offer consumers in world markets much more for less (Zeng and Williamson, 2007). This is translated into (1) offering consumers worldwide high technology at low cost; (2) producing a wide range of 'product varieties or customization at prices that are competitive against incumbent's standardized, mass-markets offerings'; and (3) using the Chinese low-cost 'to reduce the break-even of producing specialty products' (Williamson and Yin, 2009, p. 82).
- Combinative capabilities: 'the capability to deliver variety and customization to the global market at low cost'. This means that Chinese

companies are finding 'ways to innovate on the cheap and avoid reinventing the wheel' (Williamson and Yin, 2009, p. 83).

- Dynamic capabilities: 'high levels of flexibility, rapid learning, and the ability to deal with uncertain and ambiguous change' (Williamson and Yin, 2009, p. 84). These capabilities are mainly the result of operating in a society (and domestic market) in a constant state of flux and also of the hybrid private and state ownership that gives management more autonomy to make quick decisions and independence from short-term pressures of capital markets.

These capabilities place Chinese international firms in a good position as 'the changing demands of the global market will reward companies with the capabilities to succeed in an environment where developing markets comprise the largest and fastest growing part of world demand; acutely price and value-for-money consumers make up a significant and rising segment of developed markets; global concentration in global retailing places ever-greater cost pressures on suppliers; and increasing volatility in the global environment demands ever-greater high flexibility and risk tolerance from corporations' (Williamson and Yin, 2009, p. 80). Table 5.1 shows the top nonfinancial firms from China by foreign assets in 2008.

Prospects

A recent survey in China on the expansion of companies presented the following results (China Council for the Promotion of International Trade, 2010):

- Investments in the coming 12 months: 26% of the respondent enterprises expressed their intention to increase overseas investments, 30% will keep the current investment levels, and 43% will not make any overseas investments.
- Investments in the next two to five years: 61% of the enterprises will 'considerably increase' or 'probably increase' their overseas investments.
- Objectives for investments abroad: 30% aim at taking advantage of the preferential investment policies of host countries and to avoid the saturated domestic market in China. Other objectives chosen by 20% included (1) to acquire advanced technology and management experience, (2) to follow the partners moving overseas, and (3) to provide raw materials and natural resources for the domestic market.

Table 5.1 China's top nonfinancial firms, ranked by foreign assets, 2008[a]

Corporation	Industry [c]	Assets		Sales		Employment		TNI b
		Foreign	Total	Foreign	Total	Foreign d	Total	(Per cent)
CITIC Group	Diversified	43,750	238,725	5,427	22,230	18,305	90,650	21.0
China Ocean Shipping (Group) Company	Transport and storage	28,066	36,253	18,041	27,431	4,581	69,648	49.9
China National Petroleum Corporation	Petroleum expl./ref./distr.	9,409	264,016	4,384	165,224	20,489	10,86,966	2.7
China State Construction Engineering Corporation	Construction and real estate	7,015	29,873	3,619	29,080	15,765	113,251	16.6
Sinochem Corp.	Petroleum expl./ref./distr.	6,409	19,825	34,218	44,280	225	26,632	36.8
China National Offshore Oil Corp.	Petroleum expl./ref./distr.	5,247	59,917	4,475	28,028	1,739	51,000	9.4
China Communications Construction Co.	Construction and real estate	4,010	31,911	5,599	25,740	1,703	93,019	12.1
Beijing Enterprises Holdings Ltd.	Diversified	3,662	6,670	2,524	2,530	28,260	37,000	77.0
China Railway Construction Corporation Ltd	Construction	3,146	32,204	2,475	31,571	18,613	190,545	9.1
ZTE Corp.	Other consumer goods	3,143	7,642	3,860	6,373	19,031	61,350	44.2

Continued

Table 5.1 Continued

Corporation	Industry [c]	Assets		Sales		Employment		TNI b
		Foreign	Total	Foreign	Total	Foreign d	Total	(Per cent)
Lenovo Group	Electrical and electronic equipment	2,732	6,308	8,467	14,901	5,201	22,511	41.1
China Minmetals Corp.	Metal and metal products	2,269	13,484	4,318	26,668	798	44,425	11.6
TPV Technology Limited	Wholesale trade	2,266	3,354	6,860	9,247	19,256	28,500	69.8

Notes: [a] All data are based on the companies' annual reports unless otherwise stated.

[b] TNI, the Transnationality Index, is calculated as the average of the following three ratios: foreign assets to total assets, foreign sales to total sales and foreign employment to total employment.

[c] Industry classification for companies follows the United States Standard Industrial Classification as used by the United States Securities and Exchange Commission (SEC).

[d] In a number of cases foreign employment data were calculated by applying the share of foreign employment in total employment of the previous year to total employment of 2008.

Source: UNCTAD/Erasmus University database, 2010

The results of this survey suggest that Chinese managers seem to be waiting for the negative effects and uncertainty (consequences of the financial crisis that started between 2007 and 2008) to pass to resume investing abroad. In addition, Chinese companies are starting to see that the domestic Chinese market is beginning to be saturated for some products and as a consequence they are looking for new markets overseas.

These results are complemented by recent news that 'Chinese companies are preparing for a wave of investments in Europe in engineering and technology as part of an effort to find new markets and gain greater control of global supply chains'. They seem to be 'targeting businesses with expertise in machinery, materials and specialised components'. With these acquisitions Chinese companies expect to 'complement their expertise in low-cost manufacturing with skills higher up the value chain'. In fact, 'in the six months to the end of March 2011, Chinese businesses invested $64.3 billion in Europe in acquisitions, trade deals and loan agreements'; this is more than double the comparable figure over the previous three years (Marsh, 2011).

In addition, it has been reported that China Investment Corp (CIC), the Chinese sovereign wealth fund, will soon receive $100 billion to $200 billion in new funds from the government. One of the purposes of this is 'to set up a variety of new special-purpose funds that would invest in sectors such as energy and precious metals, as well as a foreign-exchange stabilisation fund' (Sender and Anderlini, 2011).

All in all, China's nonfinancial outbound foreign direct investment reached around $45 billion in 2009, a figure 48 times the total in 2002 according to UN figures. On top of this, 'from focusing almost exclusively on securing offshore supplies of natural resources Chinese companies are now interested in a wide range of industries, especially ones where they can acquire technology' (Sender and Anderlini, 2011).

5.3 The international expansion of Chinese SMEs[3]

The expansion of SMEs from China deserves a different analysis as they are different from big international firms. Chinese SMEs represent around 99% of companies in China, around 50% of the country's GDP, around 40% of tax revenues and more than 60% of the exports value (China Development Bank, 2010).

The development of SMEs in China has gone through three main stages (Chen, 2006; Spar and Oi, 2006). The first one, from 1978 to 1992, was characterised by strong support and encouragement from the government to establish collective and self-employed enterprises. The second stage, from 1992 to 2002, was characterised by the reform of state-owned SMEs and the encouragement of the non-public sector. The third stage began in 2002 when China passed the SMEs promotion law (Chen, 2006; Spar and Oi, 2006). In this process, led by important changes in the government's policy, two key factors for the development of SMEs in China were identified: (1) the development of township and village enterprises, and (2) the development of the non-public sector and, in particular, privately owned SMEs (Chen, 2006, p. 141).

The first factor, township and village enterprises (TVEs), are 'small manufacturing operations led frequently by local communist officials … [where] villages raise[d] money in any way they could (from retained earnings, agricultural profits and loans from local banks), and then use[d] these funds to do everything from making local crafts to manufacturing industrial equipment' with 'local authorities facilitating loans' (Spar and Oi, 2006, p. 7). 'Each township had its own rural savings and credit cooperative, which extended credit to local farmers and TVEs' (p. 11). 'Over time, the TVEs grew fiercely competitive with each other and, eventually, with the SOEs. They also became extremely successful, reinvesting their profits to fund growth' (p. 7). These enterprises have also helped in the transfer of labour from rural areas to non-agricultural sectors and especially in vehicles from the government (local and national) to achieve objectives in their reform and development strategies (Chen, 2006).

The second factor has been the development of the non-public sector and, in particular, privately owned SMEs. This can be seen especially after 2004 when China amended the constitution to grant the non-state-owned economy a legal status which reflected the size of the changes going on in the country along with the encouragement for the development of business. This new environment has helped to boost international activities from China's SMEs to the point where they are currently responsible for more than half of the country's exports. These exports provide evidence that Chinese SMEs in a relatively short period of time have been able to adapt their structures, practices and capabilities to successfully compete in world markets mainly via OEM agreements.

The internationalisation of Chinese SMEs has not been widely studied yet, although in one of the first studies on the internationalisation of Chinese SMEs (Cardoza and Fornes, 2009; Cardoza, Fornes, and Xu, 2011; Fornes, Cardoza, and Xu, 2011; Li, Fornes, and Cardoza, 2010) it is possible to find the following. First, SMEs from China seem to face fewer barriers to their international expansion than their Western counterparts, between 30% and 40% of the barriers to the internationalisation recollected by Leonidou (2004) from Western SMEs.

Second, different barriers apply to the different stages in the firms' expansion (regional, national and international). This suggests that SMEs go through a learning process as they expand their operations beyond their home market. Also, these barriers can be grouped into three main areas: (1) knowledge of international business; (2) international operations and logistics; and (3) skills and internal capabilities. This grouping shows that the barriers are related mainly to weak management skills and knowledge.

Third, different facilitators apply also to the different stages in the firms' expansion (regional, national and international). The support from the government was found to be relevant in the first regional expansion. But for the subsequent expansions to the regional and international markets, agreements with international companies and/or other private sources of funding were found to be key factors. This indicates that SMEs from China follow a push and then pull process, the first push from the government and then a pull from the international partner.

All in all, the national and international expansion of SMEs from China tells a different story than that of their MNEs counterparts. A key factor in the SMEs' expansion is the collaboration with foreign companies and/or private sources of funding. This, at the same time, creates big opportunities for Western SMEs. Many of them (with the knowledge, products and experience to succeed in competitive markets) are experiencing threats in their market share from Chinese value-for-money products, but they do not have the resources to establish a subsidiary in a low-cost location. The opportunities here to complement each party's strengths are self-evident.

5.4 Chinese dragons in Latin America[4]

The opening of Chinese business in Latin America is not a new phenomenon. Many countries like Argentina, Brazil or Peru have been receiving Chinese and their businesses for a long time. However, as shown in Chapter 3, what is new is that Latin America has become one of the main destinations for Chinese outward foreign investments in the last years (see Table 3.7). At the beginning there were speculations that these investments were mainly (or only) to exploit the natural resources abundant in the region. But then companies in other industries started to disembark in Latin American markets.

As it has been seen with most trade from China, commerce with Latin America started to grow at above average rates after China's accession to the WTO. But a strong push to this relationship seems to have happened after President Hu Jintao's visit to the region in 2004 and the string of visits from Latin American presidents to China (see Table 3.3).

The internationalisation of Chinese firms to Latin America also seems to have followed two stages. A first stage went from around 2001 to 2007 and a second stage from 2007 onwards. The first stage was dominated by Chinese SOEs looking for natural resources, presumably with a strong support from the government, and a trade surplus for South American countries. In the second stage the trade balance (especially with South American countries) has changed sides and it is currently posting a surplus for China while many privately owned companies from different industries are starting to invest in Latin America.

For the first stage the Chinese government seemed to have taken a more direct participatory approach from what has been seen in developed countries; most of the investments were committed by China's government itself (La Nación, 2004d, 2004c, 2004b, 2004a) rather than by a group of SOEs or MNEs. This suggests that the government is supporting and promoting investments beyond China's boundaries. This support outside the country can also be seen in the fact that the Chinese government is actively pursuing the signing of treaties and trade and investment agreements with Latin American and other emerging countries (ECLAC, 2007). For example, by 2006, China had signed agreements with 32 countries or groups of countries in Africa, Asia, Latin America and the southern Pacific which represented 25% of the country's total trade in 2005 (Bin, 2006).[5] This indirect support was also seen in the publishing by the Chinese government of a White Paper on Latin America (the full text can be found in Appendix 1). This was the first-ever white paper on the region and one of the first to appear in China's relations with international actors in the last decades.

During this first stage several multimillion dollar agreements were signed between Chinese SOEs and Latin American companies (mainly SOEs too). Examples of this are the agreement for up to US $2 billion to obtain financing in return for the long-term supply of copper signed between China's Minmetals and Chile's state-owned company Codelco (the world's largest producer of copper) funded by China's Development Bank; the agreement between China's Baosteel and Brazil's Vale do Rio Doce (the world's largest producer of iron ore) for US $5 billion to build a steel slab plant in South Brazil (later cancelled due to the financial crisis) or the agreement between Petróleos de Venezuela S.A. (PDVSA) and China National Petroleum Corporation (CNPC) for the creation of a US $6 billion fund to finance joint oil-related projects.

The second stage is most likely the result of efforts made by small, medium and large companies in the manufacturing sector that have been successfully exporting their products to Latin American markets. These companies are taking the next steps in their internationalisation process in the short- and mid-terms, going from exporting, to contracting and then FDI (Buckley and Casson, 1998; Buckley and Ghauri, 1993; Root, 1994). This means that Chinese MNEs are starting to acquire strategic assets and capabilities extending their value chains to Latin America with, for example, the acquisition of local brands, distribution channels or retail services to market their products.

Good examples of this are Chery, the car manufacturer from Anhui Province, that has started to assemble its QQ model in Uruguay with local partners to be sold in South America; Tiens, the pharmaceutical company from Tianjin, that has established direct sales networks in Argentina, Brazil, Colombia, Ecuador, Mexico, Peru and Venezuela; Refinex, the silicone implants company founded in Shanghai, that is selling its products throughout Latin America adapted to the size and weight of local customers or GREE, the world's largest residential air-conditioner manufacturer from Guangdong Province, that established a manufacturing facility in Brazil.

During this second stage investments by Chinese SOEs in natural resources have continued. For example, in March 2010 CNOOC purchased oil company Bridas in Argentina for an estimated US $3.1 billion. And then in October 2010 Sinopec took a minority stake in Spanish Repsol YPF's subsidiary in Brazil for US $7.1 billion to exploit its oil deposits in the South American country.

One of the few studies on the Chinese dragons in Latin America (Fornes and Butt-Philip, 2011a) showed that companies (for both, stage one and stage two) were mainly invited (pulled?) to go abroad by a Latin American partner with whom they then became engaged in JVs. Within the context of these agreements the Chinese firms then acquired the capabilities to operate in the host market. In these investments the support from the Chinese government did not seem to be present in the internationalisation process of these companies (at least in the format reported in previous studies (Buckley et al., 2007; Child and Rodrigues, 2005; Rugman and Li, 2007; Rui and Yip, 2008; Shoham and Rosenboim, 2009). This process is similar to what was found in SMEs shown above.

All in all, Chinese investments in Latin America up to 2007 seem to be mainly resource-seeking FDI, but the current trade and investment trends between the countries show that market-seeking FDI is slowly finding a place. After all, the SOEs' projects in natural resources, the investments in infrastructure and the trade agreements cannot only serve to feed China's growth with raw materials and food from Latin America, but also to improve access to Latin American markets for Chinese products.

Competition in Latin American markets

The fact that Chinese companies have displaced Mexico as the United States' main trading partner (ECLAC, 2008) tends to suggest that firms from China possess some advantages that they are now using to compete in Latin American markets, especially in the low and intermediate technology manufacturing sectors in which these countries have competing export baskets. The figures in Table 3.3, especially the growth in manufacturing exports from China, seem to confirm this advantage.

This apparent higher competitiveness in relation to Latin American companies can partly be explained by country-specific advantages, such as: (1) a higher rivalry in the domestic market (Porter, 1998) in which China 'is already a much more open economy than most emerging markets' (Blazquez-Lidoy et al., 2006) and particularly more open than most Latin American countries (maybe with the exception of Chile), (2) access to state-supported research (Child and Rodrigues, 2005; Zeng and Williamson, 2003), (3) domestic cost advantages (Rugman and Li 2007), (4) institutional factors (Buckley et al., 2007) and/or (5) economies of scale from a large domestic economy and market (Rui and Yip, 2008; Zeng and Williamson, 2003).

But what about firm-specific advantages? The trade figures and the industries/products (low and intermediate technology manufacturing) in which companies from China are gaining market share tend to suggest that the competitive capabilities of these firms are stronger than those of Latin American companies. Some of these advantages have probably been transferred to Chinese firms through OEMs or JVs (Cardoza and Fornes, 2009; Guthrie, 2005), and now China's enterprises are using this enhanced competitiveness to enter new markets in other emerging countries (Chen and Chen, 1998). Latin American companies have also taken part in arrangements similar to the OEMs or JVs (maquiladoras, for example); however, the figures in Table 3.3 suggest that firms from Latin America are a little behind their Chinese competitors.

It is early to make conclusions about the competitive performance of Chinese dragons vis-à-vis the Latin American companies as they have been competing only for a short period of time. But the emerging evidence seems to suggest that Chinese MNEs, based on both country-specific and firm-specific advantages, are stronger in the manufacturing sector and therefore are outcompeting their host country competitors.

The Spanish connection

When the China–Latin America economic relationship started to grow at the beginning of the previous decade, there was a feeling shared by many companies from Spain and also by the Spanish government that the European country would play an important role. The idea at that time was that of a 'triangulation', in which Spain would act as a bridge for China (and other Asian countries) to Latin America and vice-versa. In fact, this was one of the pillars of the Spanish government's Asia Pacific Framework Plan 2000–2002. The idea of this triangle was based, among other things, on the fact that Spanish companies are the largest European investor in Latin America (and some of the top players in their industries), which would make them a perfect match for Chinese companies looking for markets South of the US border (Santiso, 2006b).[6]

In this context, 'Telefónica seemed to be leading Spanish firms in the development of links with China. The company, which operates the largest telecommunication network in South America, signed a contract in 2004 with Huawei, the Chinese telecommunication equipment maker, to sell products through all Telefónica's subsidiaries in Latin America; in addition, Telefónica entered the capital of China Netcom Corporation [then absorbed by China Unicom], the second largest landline operator in China, and Telefónica president along with Telefónica International's president sit on the board of this company, one of the very few Europeans on the board of a Chinese company (Blazquez-Lidoy et al., 2006; El Mundo, 2007)' (Fornes and Butt-Philip, 2009, p. 24).

However, not much happened after these first movements. Asked about why the 'triangulation' idea was not working, the CEO of a Chinese company with investments in Latin America (who wants to remain anonymous) in a private meeting in 2008 said something like 'China is too big to need a bridge to reach Latin America'. Professor Jiang Shixue, deputy director of the Institute of European Studies at the Chinese Academy of Social Sciences, on the 'triangulation' idea added recently that 'in the initial stage some years ago when China and Latin America did not know each other very well, outside help would be more necessary. Now the initial stage is approaching to an end' (Shixue, 2009).

These comments seem to summarise what the evidence is showing, that the Chinese government and then Chinese companies have been arriving in Latin America almost without the help from the EU or

Spain, and also that Spanish companies are lagging behind their competitors in their trade and investments with China (Spain is only the sixth trading partner with China within the EU). The few Spanish companies currently operating in both regions (on top of Telefónica), like BBVA, Roca Sanitarios, Gamesa, Técnicas Reunidas, Indra, Sol Meliá, Santander or Telvent claimed to have entered China almost without any leverage from their positions in Latin America (Solana Gonzalez, 2008) (with the exception, of course, of the companies' size given by their investments in the region).

Nevertheless, opportunities are still arising. 'European firms have been relatively successful in their industries (financial services, energy, automotive, food, commerce, education, etc.) by commercialising in Latin America products and services previously developed mainly for the European market; now they will have to rethink their offer in order to cater for the needs of the enterprises coming from China. In this context, the strong cultural and social links between Europe and Latin America, especially with Spain, Portugal, Italy and France, have made the competition relatively easy for European companies in the host markets; nevertheless, the addition of Chinese culture to the equation gives extra complexity to already highly competitive markets. Psychic distance will work in both directions in this process. A good example of a successful adaptation to Chinese needs is Fiat's Palio, a car developed some years ago specifically for the Mercosur which was manufactured and sold in China. Another interesting example is that of Spain's business schools IE and ESIC, both have been receiving a constant flow of students from Latin America and they are now operating in China' (Fornes and Butt-Philip, 2009, pp. 24–25).

5.5 Conclusions

This chapter has shown that both the development of the Chinese dragons and their internationalisation to Latin America are processes in a constant state of flux. For this reason, it is early to make conclusions on their competitive performance vis-à-vis their Latin American counterparts, although it seems possible to say that they are strong in the low and medium technology sector, in which they are outcompeting local companies.

It will be interesting to keep a close eye in the development of the Chinese dragons in Latin America, an environment that has been described as challenging for businesses (Fornes, 2008; Fornes, 2009) and where its changing nature has affected the performance of large foreign investors (Fornes and Cardoza, 2009). In particular, Chinese dragons will likely face some of the following challenges in their operations in Latin America: (1) they will be operating in a region where the presence of ethnic Chinese networks is still low (South America may be one of the few places in the world where it is difficult to find a Chinatown!); (2) Latin America presents an important psychic distance; (3) trade and investments seem to be geographically dispersed in a large continent where communication is not easy and (4) Chinese companies tend to operate in a relatively more centralised fashion (Cai, 1999), which could eventually prevent them from making decisions locally and adapting smoothly to changes in the business environment.

6
Multilatinas and the China Challenge

The growth of Latin America depends on what happens in China.[1]

6.1 Introduction

The 'translatinas' or 'multilatinas' are companies based in a Latin American state with value-added activities outside their country of origin (Cuervo-Cazurra, 2010; ECLAC, 2006). Although they are not a new phenomenon, for example Alpargatas, Bunge and Born, or SIAM Di Tella from Argentina established foreign subsidiaries in the first part of the twentieth century, multilatinas started to gain presence and weight mainly in the last decade alongside increases in the net outward FDI from their home countries. In fact, acknowledging their growing importance, the *New York Times* in 2007 published that 'the new "multi-Latinas" are aggressive, resourceful enterprises that are a developing byproduct of the market liberalization that swept Latin American economies in the 1990s. But their broadening reach through the United States and the rest of the world – simmering below the surface for years – is beginning to turn heads' (Krauss, 2007).

The *Financial Times* in 2008 added to this that 'not so long ago, the idea that Latin American companies – traditionally cosseted, family-owned concerns or sluggish, public-sector behemoths – would start to dominate global industries would have sounded fanciful in the extreme' (Lapper and Wheatley, 2008). These comments were the result of both the rapid growth experienced by multilatinas in the last decade, and the fact that some of them have become world leaders in their sectors. Examples of this can be found in Mexico's Cemex (the world's largest building materials supplier and third largest cement producer), Brazil's

Embraer (the third largest aircraft company in the world behind Boeing and Airbus), Brazil's Vale (the largest producer of iron ore in the world) or Argentina's Techint (whose subsidiary Tenaris is the world's largest manufacturer of seamless steel tubes). What is also impressive about this rapid expansion is the shareholder value created by multilatinas: 'the total shareholder return (TSR) of the 68 multilatinas that were publicly traded over the past ten years was much higher than the TSR of the benchmark markets, including the MSCI Emerging Market Index' (Aguiar et al., 2009, p. 5) even considering the impact of the financial crisis on share prices.

A quick look at multilatinas shows that although they operate in most industry sectors their penetration varies widely. 'They have a strong presence in Latin American aerospace activities; basic materials (construction materials, pulp and paper, oil and gas, and metals and mining); transportation; media and entertainment; food and beverage; and telecommunications. But they have a negligible presence, relative to external MNCs, in automotive, technology, and even agricultural commodities' (Aguiar et al., 2009, p. 5). In addition, 'even if taken as a whole, the multilatinas are still relatively small in size and their presence in terms of countries and geographical areas is significantly inferior to that of developed countries' MNCs' (Minda, 2008, p. 21).

In any case, the emergence of the multilatinas has led to important changes in the corporate landscape of Latin America due to their size and leadership in different sectors. In addition, the growth of their international activities, which are advancing alongside the expansion of MNEs from Asian emerging economies, is not without consequences to the dynamics of the global economy and in particular to the developed economies-emerging markets relations (Minda, 2008).

6.2 Latin American companies' development and main characteristics

The development of multilatinas can be divided into three main phases. The first phase from the 1950s/1960s to the 1990s was guided by the Import Substitution Industrialisation (ISI) policies followed by their home countries. During these years, ISI reduced the pressure on companies to improve capabilities, and the international operations were mainly exports to neighbouring countries of natural resources, or civil engineering projects and their construction. The main reasons to go abroad during this period were the need to find markets for their raw materials and also to diversify the sources of supply.

The second phase started in the 1990s and it continued until around 2004. There years were dominated by the economic policies of the Washington Consensus. This period has been regarded as not positive for the region by many commentators in terms of economic growth (some even call it the 'lost half decade'), although it seems to have created the conditions for the future development of the multilatinas. The deregulation, opening of the economy and privatisations that took place during these years increased the need to improve the competitiveness of local firms as they facilitated the access to foreign competitors. For example, between 1991 and 2001 the number of state-controlled firms in Latin America fell from 20% to less than 9%. Probably for the first time, domestic enterprises found themselves confronted with Western MNEs and also competed against Asian companies.

The last years of this phase were influenced by the Asian crisis that started in 1997 and the crisis in Brazil and Argentina in 2000 and 2001 respectively that resulted in a FDI downturn and an economic slowdown in the region. Two important events were observed during this period: (1) several foreign MNEs abandoned the region and sold off their investments in the belief that the poor economic situation and business environment would continue, making it difficult to continue operating in Latin America and (2) local companies took the opportunity to buy these devalued assets from their (until then) competitors in the local market, which helped them to consolidate their position in the domestic and regional markets.

The transition to the third phase from 2004 onwards was dominated by a drastic reduction in the cost of capital (currently there are five investment-grade countries, Mexico, Brazil, Chile, Colombia[2] and Peru which together represent around 75% of the region's nominal GDP). In fact, experts attribute the growth of multilatinas mainly to Latin America's improving economic prospects, which have made it easier for companies to raise capital cheaply. Since the Tequila crisis in Mexico in 1994 that saw a default in the country's sovereign debt and an important devaluation in the currency, most governments in Latin American states have been cautious in their fiscal and monetary policies. This has resulted in low inflation, a steady fall in the domestic interest rate, surpluses in the current account, increases in central bank reserves, flexible exchange rates and better access to credit. In addition, companies in some of the region's countries can issue debt in local currency, an option that was not available before the start of the twenty-first century (Robledo, 2010). These years also saw the development and growth of the Latibex which, based in the Madrid Stock Exchange, allows Latin

American companies to trade their shares and securities in a European stock market (see Appendix 2 for more details).

About this, Hector Medina, finance director of Cemex, remembers that 'during the 1980s and 1990s, most international businesses from Latin America paid much more than their international rivals to finance overseas expansion'. For example, Cemex 'paid in the region of 12% on bonds issued to finance its first wave of international expansion at the end of the 1980s'. By contrast, the company 'is able to finance plans now at only about 4 %, a rate as good as or better than that available to rivals from developed countries' (quoted in [Lapper and Wheatley, 2008]).

Two more elements have dominated this third phase: the sharp rise in the price of commodities, and the management skills and international vision of the senior management teams. The combination of these elements with the lower cost of capital resulted in aggressive companies with strong balance sheets (in particular comfortable cash positions) that encouraged a trend of large scale acquisitions. A good example of the magnitude of these operations was Vale's 2008 US $85 billion attempted bid for its Anglo-Swiss rival Xstrata. This M&As-driven expansion strategy that was followed by some multilatinas has resulted in an increase in the number of companies from Latin America among the world's largest companies. In fact, the Fortune 500 ranking for 2009 included eleven companies from Latin America (compared to five in 2005), of which Brazil accounted for six. However, it is important to recognise that 'in terms of the biggest multinationals from the developing world, Latin America is still dwarfed by other regions such as East Asia' (Oxford Analytica, 2010).

Multilatinas have generally moved out of their 'conglomerate' approach of the past to a more focused business model in which companies in a group are generally interconnected and make better business sense. In the past, multilatinas were generally highly leveraged. But now they have a strong capital position and treat debt with respect, probably derived from the lessons learned during successive Latin American financial crises (Rovzar, 2009). Most multilatinas have fuelled their growth by resorting to equity markets, and they are also leveraging their acquisitions to support their overseas expansion (Aguiar et al., 2009). Figure 6.1 shows the three phases described previously linked to the level of net outward FDI from Latin America and the Caribbean countries (in the y axis).

The growth and development of the multilatinas have continued alongside the net outward FDI from the region which has maintained

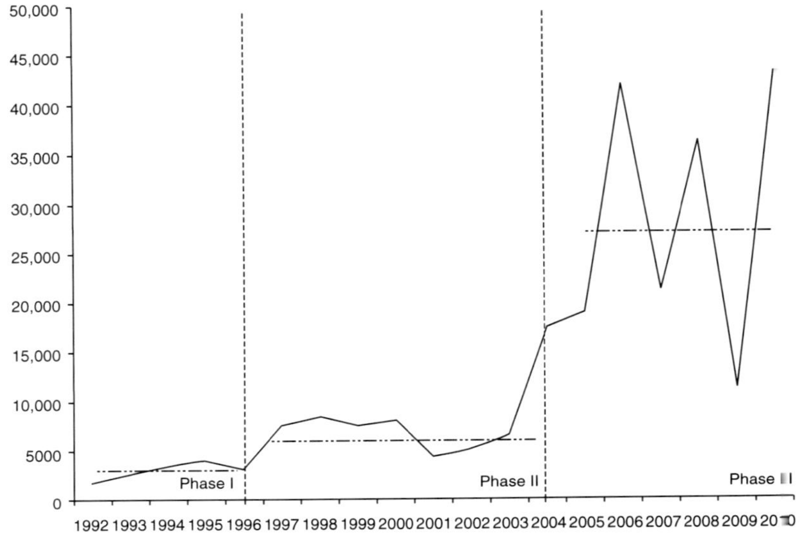

Figure 6.1 Latin American and the Caribbean net outward FDI, 1992–2010 in millions of US dollars
Source: ECLAC, 2011b.

an average of around 5% of the world's total (Cuervo-Cazurra, 2010). The average outward FDI from 2004 to 2010 was US $26 billion per year, and in 2010 it reached a record US $43.1 billion which represented 17% of the total FDI from developing countries (ECLAC, 2011b). Table 6.1 presents the outward FDI from Latin America and the Caribbean from 2000 to 2010. In this table it is possible to observe that the investments abroad of Peruvian companies in 2010 is ten times larger than the 2000–2005 average; the same comparison in other countries shows that the international investments for Colombian companies is six times larger, and it is five times larger for Brazilian, Chilean and Mexican firms (it is not a coincidence that these are the only investment-grade countries in the region, which provides low-cost capital to fund the expansion of their companies).

During these years most multilatinas have expanded internationally to their 'natural markets'; markets with geographical proximity, a similar linguistic sphere and common historical links, to increase their levels of comfort and leverage their value proposal with the familiarity with the tastes of the consumers in the host markets (Casanova and

Table 6.1 Latin America and the Caribbean net outward FDI, 2000–2010, in alphabetical order, in billions of US dollars

Country	2000–2005[a]	2006	2007	2008	2009	2010
Argentina	532	2439	1504	1391	710	946
Barbados	3	44	82	63	41	0
Belize	0	8	7	10	4	3
Bolivia	1	3	4	5	−4	0
Brazil	2513	28202	7067	20457	−10084	11500
Chile	1882	2171	2573	8040	8061	8744
Colombia	1156	1098	913	2254	3088	6504
Costa Rica	17	98	263	6	7	9
El Salvador [b]	15	−26	100	16	23	80
Guatemala	31	40	25	16	23	29
Honduras	4	1	1	−1	1	1
Jamaica	84	85	115	76	61	0
Mexico [c]	3491	5758	8256	1157	7019	12694
Paraguay	5	4	8	8	0	0
Peru	22	0	66	736	398	215
Trinidad and Tobago	146	370	0	700	0	0
Uruguay	15	−1	89	−11	2	−6
Venezuela	809	1524	30	1273	1834	2390
Total	**10726**	**41818**	**21103**	**36196**	**11184**	**43109**

Notes: [a]: Simple average
[b]: The 2010 data cover up to the third quarter
[c]: The average shown for the first half of the decade corresponds to 2001–2005

Source: ECLAC, 2011b

Fraser, 2008). In this context, the main targets have been the Hispanic population in the United States where companies like Televisa or Pollo Campero are successfully commercialising their TV programmes and fried chicken. Other targets are Spain and Portugal as gateways to the EU like Gerdau in steel or Odebrecht in construction (Barciela, 2011; Casanova and Fraser, 2008). In addition, companies are taking advantage of the FTAs functioning in the Americas. Mexican companies are increasingly investing in the United States and Canada within the framework provided by the NAFTA, and Brazilian companies are acquiring assets in Argentina within the context of the Mercosur. Chilean companies have also been very active in the region. Firms like CMPC, Falabella, LAN or Cencosud saw their growth limited by a small domestic market and were one of the first to invest in their neighbours within the context of the FTAs signed with the Mercosur and most American countries (including the United States and Canada).

As stated at the beginning of this chapter, multilatinas have brought important changes to the Latin American business landscape. The first of these changes can be seen in the development, growth and consolidation of regional brands. Names like LAN, Claro, Bimbo, Taca, Falabella, Natura or Marcopolo, among many others, are now easily found in airports, billboards, supermarkets or shopping centres across Latin America. The second important change has been the increase in the intratrade among Latin American countries. This can be seen in Table 6.2 that presents the intraregional exports as a percentage of total exports. In this table it is possible to see that the share of intraregional trade has grown 46% (from 13% to 19% of the total trade) from 1990 to 2009, with countries like Ecuador, El Salvador or Nicaragua increasing their share more than 20 points, and other countries like Argentina, Bolivia, Brazil, Colombia, Costa Rica, Dominican Republic, Guatemala and Honduras increasing their share more than 10 points. The third change is a byproduct of the second; Mexico has increased its share of intraregional trade almost 100%, from 3% in the period of 1999–2004 to 7% in 2008 and 6% in 2009. This is likely the consequence of stronger competition in the United States, the main destination for its exports, due to the increasing presence of Chinese firms as presented in Chapter 3.

Drivers for the multilatinas' expansion

Three main drivers supporting the regional and then international expansion of Latin American firms can be identified:

- The changes in the business environment that started with the structural reforms of the 1990s 'induced firms to develop their ownership advantages to operate in a higher-competition environment' (Cuervo-Cazurra, 2008, p. 149). This also resulted in an important liberalisation of the Latin American economy (measured by the openness ratio, it went from 12% to 21% of the region's GDP from the 1990s to 2006 (Casanova and Fraser, 2008) and sound economic policies in most countries, especially after the 1994 Tequila crisis in Mexico and the 2000/2001 Samba and Tango crises in Brazil and Argentina. One of the most celebrated consequences of these policies was the drastic reduction in the cost of capital for firms which, at the same time opened the door to access the largest financial markets in the world through the American Depository Receipts (ADRs) or the Latibex (see Appendix 2 and Appendix 3 for more details). In this sense an important milestone was the ADR programme launched by Compañía de

Table 6.2 Latin America and the Caribbean intraregional exports, percentages of intraregional exports with respect to total exports calculated on the basis of FOB exports

Country	1990	1991	1992	1993	1994	1995	1996	1997	1998	1999	2000	2001	2002	2003	2004	2005	2006	2007	2008	2009
Argentina	26	29	33	41	45	47	47	50	50	45	48	46	42	38	40	40	42	40	39	42
Bahamas[c]	1	1	2	n/a	n/a	n/a	n/a	1	1	1	8	1	2	2	1	1	3	2	4	n/a
Barbados[c]	17	23	21	27	23	26	36	30	31	31	24	33	26	21	27	18	17	41	16	22
Belize[c]	10	8	9	7	8	8	4	6	9	7	7	9	8	12	14	16	25	40	26	n/a
Bolivia	45	48	39	37	39	37	48	43	44	38	45	59	60	64	65	67	66	62	65	60
Brazil	11	17	22	25	24	23	24	27	27	23	25	22	18	20	23	25	26	25	24	21
Chile	13	15	17	20	21	19	20	21	24	22	22	24	20	19	18	17	17	17	19	18
Colombia	16	22	24	26	22	28	27	28	29	25	29	35	32	29	33	34	31	36	36	31
Costa Rica	17	17	22	22	21	21	21	21	26	16	19	23	24	23	26	25	18	25	28	27
Cuba[a]	n/a	n/a	n/a	n/a	n/a	n/a	n/a	n/a	n/a	10	10	9	10	19	22	26	53	56	n/a	n/a
Dominican Republic[c]	3	3	2	2	2	3	2	2	12	16	14	16	4	8	5	5	7	12	17	20
Ecuador	18	17	18	21	22	22	24	25	26	27	32	32	28	29	34	31	27	33	36	42
El Salvador	35	39	54	49	50	48	51	48	56	61	61	69	70	70	65	65	64	66	66	67
Guatemala	35	39	41	41	45	40	41	40	42	44	41	53	49	53	56	52	47	55	55	52
Guyana[c]	12	5	6	n/a	n/a	n/a	n/a	n/a	n/a	n/a	14	18	18	19	19	19	19	20	15	14
Haiti	1	0	1	0	0	0	1	0	n/a	n/a	n/a	n/a	n/a	n/a	n/a	n/a	n/a	n/a	n/a	n/a
Honduras	7	7	8	10	9	12	13	13	22	28	26	19	31	29	27	24	19	31	38	25
Jamaica[c]	6	6	6	6	7	n/a	4	4	4	4	6	5	6	5	5	4	4	3	4	6
Mexico[b]	6	7	5	5	4	5	5	5	4	3	3	3	3	3	3	5	5	6	7	6
Nicaragua	22	26	28	27	30	22	20	23	28	34	32	41	52	44	42	43	23	45	44	48
Panama	18	21	17	20	19	20	20	22	23	24	23	23	27	18	17	19	19	16	16	19
Paraguay	52	47	50	49	58	65	70	57	59	48	75	65	69	65	59	58	59	63	69	n/a

Continued

Table 6.2 Continued

Country	**1990**	**1991**	**1992**	**1993**	**1994**	**1995**	**1996**	**1997**	**1998**	**1999**	**2000**	**2001**	**2002**	**2003**	**2004**	**2005**	**2006**	**2007**	**2008**	**2009**
Peru	15	18	20	19	19	17	17	17	18	16	18	20	17	18	20	21	21	21	21	16
Suriname[c]	6	11	12	n/a	8	8	5	5	6	n/a	6	7	10	10	11	10	11	9	14	n/a
Trinidad and Tobago[c]	14	19	20	24	27	32	29	33	36	33	31	34	27	25	17	26	20	20	26	19
Uruguay	40	41	42	51	54	53	54	56	63	53	54	51	42	41	36	35	37	41	40	39
Venezuela	9	13	17	20	28	28	19	22	27	20	20	19	20	15	18	13	14	n/a	n/a	n/a
Total Region	**13**	**16**	**17**	**19**	**19**	**20**	**19**	**20**	**20**	**16**	**16**	**17**	**15**	**15**	**16**	**17**	**17**	**19**	**20**	**19**

Notes: [a]: Preliminary figures.
[b]: Starting from 1992, the data supplied by Mexico include goods processed under maquila arrangements
[c]: Some years include re-exports.
Source: ECLAC, 2010d

Teléfonos de Chile (CTC, currently a subsidiary of Spain's Telefónica) in the 1990s, the first ever from a Latin American company.

- The management skills and international vision and ambition of the senior managers and owners of the multilatinas. In particular, 'the pragmatic knowledge of complex political and regulatory environments' along with the 'lessons learned from domestic competition with foreign MNCs' (Casanova and Fraser, 2008, p. 23). This also includes the opportunistic acquisitions of industrial assets when foreign MNCs were leaving the region due to unstable political and economic conditions.
- The combination of a relatively uniform Latin American market (in terms of language and historical roots), the companies' experience in serving low-income and price-sensitive consumers, and their familiarity to deal with difficult distribution systems. These factors that once were barriers to the development of Latin American companies are now one of the sources of competitive advantages; evidence of this is the wide range of regional brands covering the southern states of the United States to the city of Ushuaia in Argentina's Patagonia.

Main characteristics of multilatinas[3]

Mutlilatinas share the following three characteristics:

- 'Ownership: multilatinas are owned predominantly by private investors (97%) and controlled by individual families (77%). In contrast, Russian multinationals, for example, are 33% government owned, and Chinese multinationals are 69% government owned. An important implication is that multilatinas are largely unaffected by governmental or geopolitical objectives. In addition, concentrated ownership often confers an agility advantage, which can be crucial, for example, in M&A activities.
- Regional focus: multilatinas are largely regional contenders, focused on their natural markets in the Americas (although many of them also operate farther afield). Argentina, the United States and Peru are the primary destinations for multilatinas' international expansion; 53%, 49% and 42% of multilatinas are active in these locations. Brazilian multilatinas are generally more focused on South American countries, and Mexican multilatinas concentrate on markets in the United States. MNEs from India and China have focused primarily on targeting developed markets in the United States and the EU, as well as developing markets.

- Industry focus: multilatinas are present in a balanced mix of industries, whereas MNEs based in other EMs tend to be more concentrated in narrower bands of industries and also have more representatives in technology sectors.' (Aguiar et al., 2009, p. 9)

Table 6.3 presents Latin America's top firms. The companies are ranked by a Globalisation Index developed by América Economía which includes sales, investments and employees abroad, along with the number of regions/countries where the firm operates and the company's growth potential. As can be seen, the list is dominated by 27 Brazilian multilatinas, followed by 15 from Mexico, and Chile is in third place with 11 companies.

An interesting observation from this table is the fact that the top ten in the list receives, on average, 72% of their sales from abroad, invests 67% outside their home country and 61% of their employees are based overseas. The averages for the top 20 show that 62% of sales come from abroad, 59% of the investments are carried out outside their home country and 58% of their employees are based overseas. This suggests that, although there are only a few multilatinas among the world's largest companies, the big multilatinas have a global reach similar to that of their counterparts.

6.3 The multilatinas and China

Although some multilatinas have succeeded in their internationalisation process by specialising or intensifying their activities in manufactured products based on natural resources like cement, petrochemicals and pulp (UNCTAD, 2006), it has been long recognised that in general, Latin America suffers from a problem of competitiveness when compared with Asia as the rates of accumulation of physical and human capital are relatively lower resulting in a low productivity of factors and less innovation capacity (Maloney and Perry, 2005). For this reason the multilatinas need to continue diversifying their exports (from the traditional commodities like iron, oil, soya etc.) as they have been doing in the last two decades (when the commodities' share of total exports was reduced from 50% to less than 30% [Schwab, 2006]) if they want to continue growing sustainably. However, the demand from China, mainly for natural resources, seems not to be helpful for this purpose. China has replaced the United States as the main destination for Brazilian oil and it is also a leading destination for Brazilian soybeans and chemical wood pulp, but the demand for passenger cars, Brazil's main manufactured export, seems to be small in the Asian country (Romei and Wheatley, 2010). This can be seen in Figure 6.2, Brazilian exports by sector; in this figure it is possible to see that primary goods exports to China have been replacing the sales abroad of manufactured goods, especially after 2007 (see also Box 3.3).

In addition, a recent study (Gallagher and Porzecanski, 2010) showed that Chinese manufacturing exports are becoming a big threat for Latin American manufactures in world markets with 92% of Latin America's manufacturing exports under threat from China by 2009, a share that represents 39% of Latin America's total exports and with Brazilian exports being one of the most heavily exposed (Gallagher, 2010). But this needs to be considered along with the foreign exchange policies followed by China and Latin American countries in the last years; while China has pegged the renminbi to a devaluing US dollar, most Latin American countries with flexible/free foreign exchange regimes have seen the value of their currencies increasing vis-à-vis the greenback. For example, the rise in commodity exports has appreciated the Brazilian real around 40% in the last two years (Leahy, 2011d). This prompted Guido Mantega, Brazil's finance minister, to say in 2010 that the world is in the midst of an international currency war and as a consequence he called for a revaluation of the renminbi (Leahy, 2011c; *The Economist*, 2010; Webb, 2010); it also prompted Dilma Rousseff, Brazil's president, to raise the issue of China's allegedly undervalued currency in her first visit to Beijing since taking office in April 2011 (Leahy, 2011a) as domestic companies are feeling the pressure from Chinese manufactured imports (Leahy, 2011d; Pearson, 2011b).

Despite of the current situation with the value of currencies, multilatinas can leverage their expansion to China on a set of competitive capabilities. For example, an advantage they have over other non-Latin American multinationals is that their management teams have experienced two or three financial crises before (Fornes, 2009) which 'gives them a competitive advantage over some of the firms they compete with whose management may not be as well versed on crisis management' (Rovzar, 2009). In addition, multilatinas have internationalised their operations while developing their competitive capabilities, a process dubbed co-evolution (Cuervo-Cazurra, 2002, 2010). This has resulted in sophisticated companies, more than what is usually thought (Cuervo-Cazurra, 2008), with capabilities to develop technological innovations, efficient organisational structures and effective social corporate responsibility programmes that match those of their Western counterparts. In

Table 6.3 Latin America's top firms, ranked by a Globalisation Index developed by América Economía, sales in millions of US dollars

Rank 2011	Rank 2010	Company	Country	Sector	Sales 2010	Number of countries 2010	Foreign sales % 2010	Overseas investments % 2010	Employees overseas % 2010	Potential growth index 2010	Globalisation index 2010
1	4	Brightstar	Bo	Telecommunications	6400.0	61	60.3	76.0	84.0	83.7	82.3
2	1	Grupo JBS (Friboi)	BR	Food	28417.6	21	89.2	65.5	64.0	92.3	78.2
3	3	Cemex	MX	Cement	14434.5	35	75.6	67.7	65.8	80.0	77.7
4	2	Tenaris	AR	Steel	7711.0	11	80.4	81.0	71.7	77.0	77.0
5	6	Lan	CL	Airlines	4387.1	19	78.0	76.4	43.0	78.0	73.2
6	10	Telmex	MX	Telecommunications	8132.5	9	94.9	50.2	92.2	81.0	70.0
7	5	Grupo Alfa	MX	Spare parts – petroch.	11044.5	17	54.0	71.0	51.5	72.0	69.8
8	–	IMPSA (Pescarmona)	AR	Energy	788.9	11	84.0	78.0	65.0	58.5	69.0
9	7	Vale	BR	Mining	49949.0	38	33.6	49.8	27.1	94.0	67.2
10	9	Const. Norberto Odebrecht	BR	Engineering	5500.0	34	70.5	56.0	48.6	67.0	66.3
11	8	Gerdau	BR	Steel	18841.2	14	38.9	59.9	48.0	82.0	65.1
12	14	Ajegroup	PE	Beverages	1127.0	16	78.0	67.3	74.0	47.0	64.0
13	11	Grupo Bimbo	MX	Food	9487.2	18	55.0	60.1	52.7	69.0	63.8
14	12	Petrobras	BR	Oil	128000.0	28	34.5	31.0	19.9	99.3	61.3
15	31	Avianca – Taca	co/ES	Airlines	3000.0	23	82.0	22.0	77.0	79.7	61.3
16	–	Laboratorios Bagó	AR	Pharmaceuticals	654.5	18	23.1	85.0	69.0	40.0	60.3
17	13	América Móvil	MX	Telecommunications	49220.6	18	36.0	33.0	70.0	87.0	60.2
18	22	Grupo Nac. De Chocolates	CO	Food	2224.9	11	38.0	71.6	19.5	67.0	59.1

19	**45**	Grupo Casa Saba (Fasa)	MX	Retail	4100.0	4	73.0	53.0	70.0	69.3	58.8
20	**15**	Marfrig	BR	Food	7788.1	22	54.9	31.6	41.7	72.0	57.0
21	**17**	Sudamericana De Vapores	CL	Shipping	5448.1	6	93.4	37.4	63.0	52.0	54.1
22	**20**	Cencosud	CL	Retail	11822.2	5	56.0	48.3	55.6	66.0	54.0
23	**16**	Camargo Corrêa Cimentos	BR	Cement	1663.2	4	51.0	66.0	56.7	51.7	53.7
24	**28**	Brasil Foods	BR	Food	12741.8	25	41.9	16.0	17.0	82.3	53.7
25	**19**	Interoceánica	CL	Shipping	821.9	4	79.2	58.0	54.0	40.0	53.7
26	**21**	Mexichem	MX	Petrochemicals	2953.7	15	76.2	30.1	70.0	57.0	53.7
27	**37**	Viña Concha y Toro	CL	Beverages	798.6	28	81.5	19.4	13.4	69.0	52.7
28	**25**	Sonda	CL	Technology	951.9	9	55.3	42.0	79.5	49.0	51.7
29	**35**	Gruma	MX	Food	3761.3	14	66.9	18.4	62.6	59.0	51.2
30	**18**	Embraer	BR	Aerospace	5216.2	5	93.0	26.5	11.0	69.0	50.6
31	**36**	Arauco	CL	Wood/cellulose	3788.4	10	87.0	23.3	21.6	64.0	50.2
32	**43**	Fibria	BR	Cellulose	3771.1	7	44.0	28.0	4.0	77.0	49.8
33	**32**	CMPC	CL	Wood/cellulose	3817.9	9	72.5	30.0	33.0	63.5	49.6
34	**24**	Weg	BR	Machinery	2629.2	47	26.5	19.2	14.9	65.0	48.6
35	**27**	Votorantim Cimentos	BR	Cement	5315.6	4	35.0	49.0	36.0	56.7	48.3
36	**30**	Pollo Campero	GU	Food	400.0	13	72.0	10.1	76.5	54.7	48.3
37	**26**	PDVSA	VE	Oil	95529.9	10	95.2	5.2	5.6	77.0	48.2
38	**44**	Tam	BR	Airlines	6811.8	13	31.3	9.0	8.3	87.0	48.0

Continued

Table 6.3 Continued

Rank 2011	Rank 2010	Company	Country	Sector	Sales 2010	Number of countries 2010	Foreign sales % 2010	Overseas investments % 2010	Employees overseas % 2010	Potential growth index 2010	Globalisation index 2010
39	29	Falabella	CL	Retail	8086.1	4	39.5	39.6	41.0	68.0	48.0
40	–	Grupo Argos	CO	Cement	1594.0	6	44.0	32.1	35.0	67.5	47.6
41	41	Grupo Modelo	MX	Beverages	6884.3	22	47.0	15.6	2.9	72.0	47.0
42	59	Tigre (Tubos De Conexión)	BR	Construction equip.	1280.0	9	22.4	43.2	24.7	55.7	46.2
43	–	Suzano Papel e Celulose	BR	Cellulose	2709.1	8	71.0	10.2	5.2	69.0	45.8
44	53	Metalfrio	BR	Appliances	470.2	6	36.5	41.0	50.0	38.0	45.3
45	46	P.I. Mabe	MX	Cellulose	280.0	18	46.1	36.2	24.1	41.7	44.5
46	39	Arcor	AR	Food	2386.7	16	16.3	27.2	30.0	57.0	44.3
47	34	Itaú – Unibanco	BR	Bank	46316.9	12	12.0	3.8	9.8	85.3	43.6
48	50	Grupo Televisa	MX	Media	4684.9	8	16.8	22.1	11.0	78.0	42.9
49	38	Grupo Elektra	MX	Retail	3726.3	8	15.0	28.4	17.6	72.0	42.9
50	33	FEMSA	MX	Beverages	13741.5	9	44.4	18.0	33.4	64.3	42.6
51	23	Grupo Camargo Corrêa	BR	Construct – Engin.	9698.0	14	18.4	15.0	22.5	67.0	42.4
52	40	Vitro	MX	Glass	1885.5	10	56.1	15.8	17.0	54.0	41.9

53	**42**	Andrade Gutierrez	BR	Construct – Engin.	10895.3	13	25.2	7.5	9.7	75.0	41.7
54	**60**	Artecola	BR	Chemicals	378.0	6	28.0	29.8	21.0	53.7	39.4
55	–	Copa Airlines	PA	Airlines	1411.1	7	25.3	18.0	24.0	56.0	39.2
56	**47**	Madeco	CL	Wood/cellulose	338.8	3	58.6	17.0	50.7	55.5	39.2
57	**52**	Cía. Siderurgica Nacional	BR	Steel	8300.6	3	26.2	13.4	7.3	68.0	37.9
58	**56**	Natura	BR	Cosmetics	3082.9	9	7.2	7.6	26.7	65.0	37.8
59	–	Bematech	BR	Technology	199.5	25	13.6	15.0	8.3	45.0	37.4
60	**54**	Marcopolo	BR	Auto spare parts	1779.2	7	18.0	11.3	31.6	53.0	35.7
61	**55**	Grupo Gloria	PE	Food	817.0	6	16.3	14.2	24.0	61.0	35.7
62	**49**	Lupatech	BR	Engineering	349.0	38	23.6	13.7	26.2	54.0	34.8
63	–	Totvs	BR	Technology	677.9	19	3.8	2.8	7.4	54.0	34.2
64	–	DHB Compon. Automotivos	BR	Auto spare parts	169.7	25	10.5	3.6	1.6	50.0	34.1
65	–	Cinépolis	MX	Entertainment	787.5	10	5.0	7.5	6.0	66.0	33.9
66	**57**	Ripley	CL	Retail	2122.8	2	27.0	28.2	29.0	49.0	33.7

Source: América Economía, 2011.

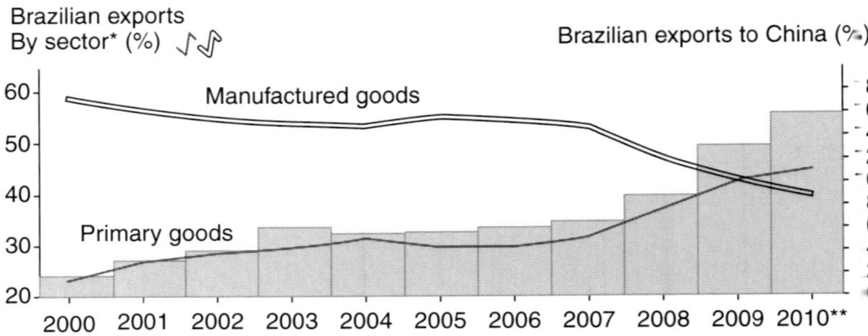

Figure 6.2 Brazilian exports by sector, in percentage, 2000–2010

Notes: *Does not include semi-manufactured goods.

**Jan–Sep

Source: Romei and Wheatley, 2010.

fact, the myth that 'Latin American companies cannot compete at the international level' is completely wrong (Cuervo-Cazurra, 2010, p. 30).

The strength of these capabilities to successfully compete in China can be seen in companies like Brazil's Embraer that set up a joint venture with China's AVIC II called Harbin Embraer Aircraft Industry Company to manufacture its ERJ 135/140/145 family aircraft (Embraer, 2002); Argentina's IMPSA that supplied four 122 MW turbines for the Dahua Hydropower dam in South China as early as 1999; Mexico's Cemex that has announced a shares issue to strengthen its presence in China (CNNExpansion.com, 2011) after receiving the 2010 Qingdao Construction Quality Management Award; Guatemala's Pollo Campero that opened its first restaurant in Shanghai in 2007 (Casanova and Hoeber, 2008); or Chile's Concha y Toro winery whose wine Trivento Golden Reserve (produced in Mendoza, Argentina) was awarded the gold medal in the 2003 China Wine and Spirits Competition (Casanova and Molina, 2008).

All in all, the multilatinas seem to be in the early process of their internationalisation although they have rapidly acquired strong positions in foreign markets. This process has been based on a set of capabilities developed mainly during the years of the Washington Consensus when their economies opened to foreign competition and also as a consequence of having dealt with two or three financial crises. The improvements in the economic conditions in most countries, mainly in the last 10 to 15 years, led to a drastic reduction in the cost of capital (now similar to that in developed economies) which triggered a wave of M&As and organic expansion first to their natural markets and now going to China.

6.4 Conclusions

Similar to what was concluded in **Chapter 5** on the Chinese dragons, this chapter has also shown that the multilatinas' expansion process is in a constant state of flux. For this reason, as seen also in **Chapter 5**, it is early to make conclusions on their competitive performance vis-à-vis their Chinese counterparts. However, a first comparison between Chinese and Latin American companies seems to suggest that, while companies from China are strong in the low and medium technology sector, firms from Latin America are strong in low price (compared to Western MNEs) advanced manufactures like airplanes or hydropower turbines as shown by the companies in the previous section.

In any case, it is possible to foresee that multilatinas will find big challenges in their operations in China; probably the most difficult will be the psychic distance (Johanson and Vahlne, 1977) as China and Latin America are too diverse. However, to their advantage it can be said that the multilatinas are used to operating in geographically dispersed fragmented markets and also dealing with rapidly changing business environments.

7
US and European Perspectives

> What we are doing hasn't worked very well and, in fact, if you look at the gains, particularly in Latin America, that Iran is making and China is making it is quite disturbing.
> I have to say that I don't think – in today's world that is a multi-polar world where we are competing for attention and relationships with at least the Russians, the Chinese and the Iranians – that it is in our interests to turn our backs on countries in our own hemisphere.
>
> Secretary of State Hilary Clinton speaking to Foreign Service Officers at the State Department, 1 May 2009.

7.1 Introduction

The aim of this chapter is to analyse from various regional perspectives the rapidly strengthening trade, investment and other economic ties that are in evidence between the People's Republic of China and Latin America and the Caribbean. Historians, as well as policy-makers, are taken aback at the speed of change of China's fortunes.

At the start of the twentieth century China had slipped into a position of economic, financial and military dependency vis-à-vis the Western powers – a position that was graphically illustrated by the massive international and military intervention which was organised to suppress the Boxer rebellion of 1898 to 1901 (Ferguson, 2011). A century later and it is clear that 500 years of Western ascendancy over China is rapidly eroding. Some recent forecasts suggest that the size of China's GDP will exceed that of the United States by around 2020. It would then also be the largest economy in the world, a position held hitherto by the United States without a break since 1872 (Ferguson, 2011). The imperatives of Chinese industrialisation (not least to secure supplies of vital commodities) are forcing China 'more or less reluctantly into.....an informal imperial strategy' (Ferguson, 2011). From a narrowly economic point of view, 'it is clearly rational for China to diversify out of dollar denominated reserves into commodity producing assets. That...has been the strategy in Beijing for some years now' (Ferguson, 2011).

7.2 Reactions from the United States

Ever since the Monroe doctrine (December, 1823) formalised the claim of US hegemony in the New World, the United States' relations with Central and Southern America have been troubled. China's new set of relationships with Latin American states does not carry the historical baggage that US political interference and US firms' economic exploitation in the region still carry. The Monroe doctrine essentially asserted US hegemony over the entire western hemisphere and was designed to warn European powers (Spain in particular) that any intervention by them in the hemisphere to protect or to restore a European (colonial) political system would be treated as a threat to the security and interests of the United States.

Nearly two centuries later the political hegemony of the United States in the western hemisphere would appear to be in marked decline as the remarks made by US Secretary of State Hilary Clinton quoted at the outset of this chapter make abundantly clear. In the last 50 years there have been military interventions of differing sizes and scales in Cuba, Nicaragua, Panama and Grenada. But it is now doubtful whether any more such interventions will take place in future.

The economic hegemony of the United States in the western hemisphere is also in marked decline in the twenty-first century; however, most Latin American exports still go to the United States and most Latin American imports come from the United States. This applies more for Central America than for South America (see Tables 6.1 and 6.2). There are clearly still significant American interests at stake in the region. The 20-year long saga of the struggle by Latin American interests to change the EU's new regime governing the trade in imported bananas – discriminatory as it was regarding Latin American producers, but protective of high cost Caribbean producers – revealed much about the state of play between the United States and Latin American or Caribbean states (Butt-Philip, 2004). The position of dominance occupied by

US-led multinationals, such as Dole, Chiquita and Del Monte, in relation to the banana trade was obvious. Yet there were some countries also involved in the dispute, such as Ecuador and Costa Rica, which were clearly determined to play an independent role in the dispute rather than always meekly follow the lead from Washington. The dispute also sharply divided Latin American and Caribbean banana producers between whom there was no love lost. The master-minding of an ultimately successful lobbying campaign on Capitol Hill, led by Chiquita's Carl Lindner, also showed how US politics is amenable to pressure from American companies with strong Latin American interests. In the end it was the appeal to the World Trade Organisation by the United States and Ecuador among others that forced the EU to back down, but the last stages of the saga were only concluded in 2010.

7.3 The European Union perspective

The European Union began its existence as the European Coal and Steel Community (1951) and it was formed by six neighbouring states including France, Germany and Italy. It has developed into a full scale customs union and common market, starting this journey with the Treaty of Rome (1957) which set up the European Economic Community (EEC), and following on with several important treaty changes. By 2011 the EU had 27 member states, with several more states in southeastern Europe (including Turkey) forming a queue to join. In 1992 the Treaty of Maastricht was signed which formed the European Union and paved the way for the introduction of a single European currency, the euro. Seventeen EU member states had adopted the euro by the start of 2011.

In trade terms, the EU, with a population of almost 500 million, remains the largest trading bloc in the world and, because it is a customs union, joint decision-making institutions in Brussels are responsible for the operation of its external trade policy. The EU states are also by far the world's largest donors of overseas aid and are significant foreign investors as well; for example they are the largest source of FDI in Brazil which is by far the largest state in Latin America. The EU state with the greatest investment interests in South America is Spain, although it should also be borne in mind that most foreign direct investment emanates from MNEs located within the EU rather than from the EU as a collective entity.

The EU itself has a complex web of relationships which spreads across Latin America. It has trade agreements with almost all the individual states of the subcontinent, and it has had a free trade agreement with Mexico since 2000 and with Chile since 2003. It has organised periodic meetings with the Andean Pact, Mercosur and all Latin American and Caribbean states jointly. The latest all-states meeting with the EU, in Madrid in May 2010, produced a wide-ranging declaration and action plan. There is a Euro-Latin American parliamentary assembly, and the EU has created its own Latin American Investment Fund (LAIF). The EU states have also arranged for the European Investment Bank to set aside a tranche of long-term capital to be made available at very low interest rates for major Latin American projects, such as the upgrading of the telecoms infrastructure of Peru. There is also access for all developing countries in Latin America and the Caribbean to financial aid for projects from the European Development Fund.

The EU can also arrange bloc to bloc agreements. The most troublesome of these in recent years for Latin America has been the long standing agreement the EU has with 78 African Caribbean and Pacific states (ACP) which offers preferential trade access to the single European market as well as other aid and development benefits. The EU's banana trade regime, mentioned above, agreed in 1993 to take account of the profound implications for this trade of the newly completed internal frontier-free single market put the EU on a collision course with several Latin American states because it tried to tip the balance of competitive advantage in the import of bananas to the Union in favour of the ACP states (Butt-Philip, 2004). This matter ended up in the WTO trade disputes procedure by the mid-1990s, but it was only finally resolved, with the EU putting in place new WTO-compliant measures in 2010 (WTO, 2009).

The other bloc relevant to this discussion is Mercosur. The EU and Mercosur have been in discussion on and off since signing a framework agreement in 1995. Their common objective has been to negotiate a free trade agreement between the two blocs, but they have not been able to come to terms. The negotiations were broken off in 2007, but it was agreed at the 2010 Madrid summit to reopen these talks. Clearly the EU's firm liberalisation agenda will be a difficult pill for some Mercosur states to swallow, but equally there is a great deal of frustration in South America that the workings of the EU's common agricultural policy have held back their agricultural exports to the EU – a sector in which many Latin American states hold a clear competitive advantage.

The Madrid summit of 2010, which brought together the EU and all the Latin American and Caribbean states, also spelled out the large number of policy areas in which there are common interests between the two regions to be pursued jointly – from unpunished criminality, illicit drugs and counterfeit goods to migration and climate change. It remains to be seen whether the Madrid declaration and its accompanying action plan will have any significant effect, perhaps leading to a step change in the EU's relations with Latin America and the Caribbean.

What, however, is clear is that there is a continuing bedrock of shared interests between the two regions arising from the large stock of FDI which EU interests have invested across Latin America, and the still very important share of Latin American exports and imports, for which the EU is responsible. Table 7.1 below illustrates the situation using four very different states (Argentina, Brazil, Chile and Mexico) as examples. The importance of the EU to South America as trading partners is evident, strikingly more significant for several states than is the United States. The listing of key trading partners for Mexico in contrast tells a very different story, the impact of proximity to the United States and NAFTA being overwhelming. Yet everywhere the rising profile of China as a trading partner also cannot be ignored.

Does the EU have the capacity to develop a strategic partnership that has impact with all or part of Latin America? Its leading role in international trade and its institutional strength in Brussels suggest that it most certainly has that capacity. The issue in practice is whether the EU will make such a strategic partnership a high enough priority. Spain and Portugal as members states would certainly be very supportive, but given the many problems that have landed on the EU's already loaded agenda, not the least of which is the ongoing battle to shore up its single currency, it is unlikely that other member states would wish the EU to commit very much time and effort to this purpose. The EU for the most part is still preoccupied with its own internal economic problems and immediate security threats in or close to its region, as well as with another round of membership enlargement negotiations.

7.4 Regional integration in Latin America

Regional integration has been the ambition of almost all Latin American states for many decades. A number of different arrangements have been made between various groupings of states to capture the theoretical economic benefits of regional integration – the success of the European Union inevitably being in the back of the minds of most opinion leaders and shapers in Latin America. There have been initiatives such as the Free Trade Area of the Americas (FTAA) agreement of 1994 which covered almost all of America, North and South, the Andean Pact of

Table 7.1 Trading partners of leading Latin American states in 2009

Brazil's Export Partners (%)		Brazil's Import Partners (%)	
EU-27	22.5	EU-27	23.2
China	12.6	United States	16.5
United States	10.6	China	12.8
Argentina	8.4	Argentina	8.9
Japan	2.9	Japan	4.4
Argentina's Export Partners (%)		**Argentina's Import Partners (%)**	
Brazil	20.4	Brazil	31.2
EU-27	18.5	EU-27	16.6
Chile	7.9	United States	13.5
United States	6.6	China	12.5
China	6.6	Mexico	3.0
Chile's Export Partners (%)		**Chile's Import Partners (%)**	
China	23.7	United States	16.9
EU-27	18.5	EU-27	15.6
United States	11.7	China	11.8
Japan	9.5	Argentina	10.9
S.Korea	6.0	Brazil	6.7
Mexico's Export Partners (%)		**Mexico's Import Partners (%)**	
United States	80.6	United States	49.0
EU-27	5.0	China	14.1
Canada	3.6	EU-27	11.6
Colombia	1.1	Japan	4.9
Brazil	1.1	S.Korea	4.8

Source: European Commission, 2011.

1969 and above all Mercosur; the latter two formally became a part of UNASUR in March 2011 (see Chapter 3). It is particularly the Mercosur experience, as the most developed framework for integration in South America, which requires evaluation. In the context of this work the big issue is whether the sudden strengthening of links between China and Latin America will weaken further the attempts to stimulate regional economic integration in the subcontinent.

The Mercosur has looked to the European Union for inspiration, but the circumstances in South America in the 1990s were, and remain, very different from those of post-1945 Europe, and capturing the economic benefits of regional integration has proven to be difficult. Among the differences between Mercosur and the EU is that there have not been the same historically induced pressures in South America to foster economic interdependence as the means to avoid future military conflicts between states, as was clearly the case in Western Europe. Another difference is that Mercosur is a customs union, but it is still not a common market.

The main reasons that regional economic integration has not proven to be the same catalyst for economic development in South America as it has been in Europe can be summarised as being structural differences, intergovernmentalist preoccupations of the member states and lack of pre-existing economic interdependence.

The structural differences can also be categorised in three parts: economic, because of the different levels of economic development achieved so far; institutional, because Mercosur has never had the significant supranational institutions which characterise the EU and geographical, because Brazil accounts for 80% of the bloc's population and some two-thirds of the bloc's GDP.

Since its inception, Mercosur has been loosely based on the European integration model. The Treaty of Asuncion envisaged a three-stage process of incremental integration – free trade, then customs union, then common market – as a textbook example of the regional economic integration process (Mukhametdimov, 2007). Mercosur also attempted to emulate the EU institutions which support the customs union, although the design was different, in order to ensure that the rules, norms and values needed to make a success of the process were in place and in effect (Best, 2011). In practice, Mercosur has not been able to achieve the success afforded to the EU. Mercosur has an imperfect customs union and a less than ideal free trade area (Costa, 2011). While the EU's single market has at last had relative success in eliminating non-tariff barriers to trade, Mercosur's common external tariff on goods can be levied twice – once upon entry to the bloc, and again when re-exported to another member of the bloc (Pang, 2009). The problem is that customs territories remain separate within the bloc, so goods are not as free to circulate as they are within the EU (House of Commons, 2007).

At the level of institutions, Mercosur's institutional set-up fosters, instead of complementing, intergovernmentalism (Costa, 2011). The direction and pace of integration is not framed by an equivalent body to the supranational European Commission but it is driven instead by national governments, which not only control any integrating initiatives but also all of the ensuing stages. As a result the integration process in Mercosur has depended exclusively on calculations of national interest and upon the relative power states have been able to bring to bear upon any particular issue. One example is the difficulty Mercosur has had in securing the agreement of each of its four member states to the accession to the group of Venezuela: each member state has its own agenda, but there is also a concern that the objectives of Venezuela may not be the same as those of the present bloc.

Such an intergovernmental configuration, when combined with the requirement that all decisions must be agreed unanimously by the member states of Mercosur, has resulted in constant gridlock with almost every issue on the table highly politicised (Costa, 2011). Thus while regional institutions in the EU are conceived as mechanisms to lock in and enforce the bloc's collective agreements; in Mercosur they only act as broader political arenas to further each member state's national interests.

Strong supranational institutions also developed within the EU as a result of increased and extensive exchanges between non-state actors and national governments, in which the supranational institutions were then required to adjust regional norms and regulations to the new business environment. These institutions have in turn become engines for further regional integration, as they require some degree of pooled sovereignty. Mercosur's problem is that equivalent transnational non-state actors are relatively weak and few in number, owing to the lack of economic interdependence between the member states. It is thus all the more reliant upon national governments for compliance, enforcement and adjudication (Malamud, 2008). Mercosur's parliament does strive to achieve better coordination between domestic regulations and to increase certainty when it comes to law enforcement (Pang, 2009). Nevertheless Mercosur has so far not been able to replicate the same level of cohesion or effective supranational institutions as have developed in the EU.

The history of the subcontinent helps to explain why intraregional integration has been so hard to achieve. Colonisation confined Latin America to being an exporter of primary products and an importer of manufactured goods. The result was a low diversification of production between the bloc's members, impelling a stronger orientation towards the industrialised countries of the northern hemisphere rather than any forging of trade or other economic links with their neighbours. Thus the economic motivation for regionalism at the outset was far weaker in South America than in western Europe, especially when the fact that for Brazil to capture 90% of the Uruguayan market would be the equivalent of a mere 2% domestic market expansion is taken into account (Mukhametdimov, 2007).

It is true that the timescale adopted by Mercosur for completing its single market – 11 years – is much shorter that the 54 years needed by the EU to get to this point, but then the relative lack of intraregional interest groups and economic ties generally has made such liberalisation much easier, at least on paper. The downside is that the regional market is so much less important for the individual economies of the Mercosur states that the organisation has not felt the need to put in place strong enforcement mechanisms that act to encourage compliance as well as assert regional norms that indirectly stimulate regional economic interdependence and integration. The Mercosur dispute settlement process was only invoked nine times between 1992 and 2005, while hundreds of cases were dealt with by the EU's European Court of Justice over the same period (Malamud, 2008). Without the equivalent supranational institutions Mercosur's declaration of common goals and priorities has rarely translated into concrete joint actions and projects, while resolutions, decisions or directives from Mercosur rarely find their way into national legislation.

Mercosur's small number of member states might suggest that decision making would be made easier than in the EU, but the absolute predominance of Brazil has unhinged any form of policy harmonisation (Costa, 2011). The problem lies less with the voting structure which demands unanimity than with the extreme disparity within the group of member states. For Brazil it is very difficult to match the loss of national control over domestic policies with any gains arising from regional integration induced through Mercosur. Many studies have concluded that Brazil is responsible for the maintenance of the intergovernmental structure of the Mercosur project (Mukhametdimov, 2007). Any attempt to move to supranational decision making would only end in stalemate, because the other member states would never agree to proportionate voting rights that would be bound to give Brazil a permanent majority.

In retrospect it appears that Mercosur was intentionally created and maintained as an intergovernmental organisation, as its founders did not wish to replicate the failures of previous attempts at integration in Latin America, notably that of the Andean Pact (Malamud, 2007). Mercosur has thus never been able to benefit from the neo-functionalist 'spillover' effects that have proved to be such significant drivers of European integration. Instead Mercosur has pursued its own extreme form of intergovernmentalism – 'interpresidentialism' – where presidents not only act as decision makers but also as dispute settlers and guarantors of commitments (Malamud, 2007). This approach is counterproductive for Mercosur – its interstate bargaining approach prevents any concrete institution-building or supranational delegation while also frustrating any possibility of 'spillover' effects to move the integration process forward.

The tables in Chapter 3 show beyond doubt that the major trading partners of the principal Latin American states are mostly located outside Latin America. This particular configuration of export proclivities is a legacy of the period of colonisation, but it has become ingrained in the economic systems of almost all Latin American states. It has shaped the economic development of these countries over many decades, if not centuries. The different economies of Latin America therefore depend relatively little upon trade and investment with each other, but they do rely enormously on foreign trade with and investment from states and MNEs outside their region. In short there has never existed in South America the degree of economic interdependence that could provide sufficient foundation for a successful common market, and the founders of Mercosur have ensured that it does not have the supranational institutional capacity to change this situation significantly.

7.5 Conclusions

It is important to understand this context fully before turning to consider the impact of China upon the regional economic integration process in Latin America because, given the long and persistent history of colonial-style trade and investment links between Latin America and Europe, and Latin America and North America, the arrival of Chinese traders and investors in force in the region looks very much like the arrival of a new source of 'soft imperial power' (Ferguson, 2011). This new China dimension strengthens the bilateralism which already characterises most Latin American states' foreign and external trade policies, and that in turn undermines efforts to strengthen regional integration. Such has been the growth of this trade and investment with China since the 1990s that any improvement in intraregional economic interdependence seems insignificant by contrast.

It is possible to surmise that over time China, by adopting a similar strategic approach to the region of Latin America as a whole, could achieve by accident rather than by design some of the regional economic integration that Latin American states are seeking, perhaps by pressing for measures at the regional level that might simplify or make more efficient its own economic activities or operations. So far there is absolutely no evidence that this is happening, and the verdict on China's impact on regional integration in Latin America so far is in the negative.

The strength of China's economic growth, and the corresponding need that China has for supplies of primary products and energy, are transforming the geopolitical landscape of Latin America. The United States has yet to work out a response to this challenge, while the EU is preoccupied with difficult issues that are much more immediate and closer to home. China has the power and the opportunity to pursue its own political and economic strategies in Latin America without much competition, but may sideline the attempts being made by some Latin American states to capture some of the benefits of regional economic integration by virtue of the sheer size and scale of the growth of its trade and investment positions in so many Latin American states. Like it or not, China is in a position to exercise soft 'imperial' power in this region.

8 Conclusions

> The time has come for the incumbent powers to recognise that they cannot continue to dominate the global scene.[1]

8.1 Introduction and summary

These words from Martin Wolf, associate editor and chief economic commentator at the *Financial Times*, seem to summarise what is going on in the world; evidence of these movements has been shown and analysed in the previous chapters. The analysis of China–Latin America in this work was carried out within this context. The book presented first (Chapter 2) China–Latin America in the context of the growing importance of emerging markets in the international marketplace. It continued (Chapter 3) by analysing in detail the trade and investment relations between the two regions while providing a historical context. Chapter 4 then took a political perspective and studied the rivalry–partnership relation between China and Latin America with a focus on what they are expecting to get from this engagement. Chapter 5 and Chapter 6 presented the main characteristics of the companies from each region. And finally Chapter 7 showed an outsider's view by analysing the perspectives of the United States and the EU.

The evidence presented in this book indicates that, as has been highlighted throughout the text, the growing importance of emerging markets is changing the flows, composition and direction of trade and investments. This can be seen in the fact that emerging markets are already receiving around 50% of the world's FDI with a trend to continue increasing (Table 2.4), that there are five emerging countries in the world's top ten exporters (Table 2.2 and Table 2.3, a situation completely different from that ten years ago when trade was dominated by the United States, the EU 15 and Japan), and that a strong South–South trade axis is developing between China and Latin America (Section 4.2.).

At a more micro level there is also evidence of these changes. Companies from emerging markets, China and Latin America in this case, are going international to acquire resources (raw material, knowledge, technology, capabilities, brands, etc.) and also to improve their access to markets. As presented in Chapter 5 and Chapter 6, firms from China and Latin America are gaining scale (which has led them to reduce their operating costs), strengthening their capabilities (leading to a stronger competitive position) and reducing their cost of capital (to support their international expansion); examples of companies currently competing successfully in the world markets were given in these two chapters. In this context, what seems most important to take into account is that 'the changing demands of the global market will reward companies with the capabilities to succeed in an environment where developing markets comprise the largest and fastest growing part of world demand; acutely price sensitive and value-for-money consumers make up a significant and rising segment of developed markets; global concentration in global retailing places ever-greater cost pressures on suppliers; and increasing volatility in the global environment demands ever-greater high flexibility and risk tolerance from corporations' (Williamson and Yin, 2009, p. 80). From what has been shown previously in this book, emerging markets-based companies seem to be very well placed to compete in this new environment. This leads to an important question: where are Western MNEs in this run to conquer the fastest growing markets in the world?

All in all, it seems evident from what has been shown in previous chapters that the development of the China–Latin America axis is the tip of the iceberg of an increasing weight of emerging markets in the international stage which, along with the relative decreasing relevance of the EU, the United States and Japan, is leading to a world with a more balanced configuration. Following this trend an important question appears almost instinctively: how will the world look in, let's say, 20 years when other big emerging markets (like India, Turkey or even Russia) became relevant players in world markets? It is difficult to guess an answer, although it is safe to say that the dynamics of globalisation are and will continue to be affected by the growth of emerging markets and their increasing importance in the world economy.

8.2 Flying with the dragon

It is difficult to contest that the growing importance of emerging markets is mainly due to the re-emergence of China as one of the world's largest economies after around 150 years of political and economic changes. This new relative position of China in the world has developed a big temptation to fly with the dragon, but this has also led to a question with a difficult answer: where can the dragon take you?

In the case of Latin America, the relationship with China seems to have benefited most of the region so far, although there are many question marks about the future. One of the main concerns is China's current currency policy; for example Figure 6.2 presents the case of Brazil (which is probably similar to other neighbour countries) where it is possible to see that exports to China of value-added goods from 2007 started to decline deeply. This drop in exports coincides with the financial crisis which led to a devaluation of the US dollar and the Chinese Renminbi, and an appreciation of the Latin American currencies which has led Brazil's new government to raise its voice and advocate for a change (see Section 6.3.). China has been resisting the pressure (especially from the United States) to change its currency policy, but at the same time it needs Latin America on its side to continue feeding its economic growth and also as a destination for its products. To avoid difficult times with its Latin American partners, China will probably continue offering bilateral agreements to improve the access to some value-added products from Latin America as it is currently doing with Brazil (see Box 3.3). It does not look like Latin American countries on their own have the muscle to make China change the value of the renminbi.

Another concern is regional integration in Latin America. As discussed in Section 4.2., Section 4.3. and Section 7.4., the relationship with China is not benefiting all players in the region equally. Flows of trade and investment from China are likely to continue at similar levels which will surely unveil Latin American firms' weaknesses while at the same time China's companies are strengthening their competitive position in the region. In addition, it has been argued that China's bilateralism can hinder Latin American efforts to increase their economic integration and gain more weight on the world stage. In other words, China is in Latin America to stay, and it is not clear how inside (Latin American countries) or outside (mainly the United States, the EU and Japan) players will react; or more importantly, if they have the strength to react and compete with China.

8.3 Samba, tequila and tango: how does the party continue in Latin America?

The growth of trade with China along with China's re-emergence as an economic power have flooded the treasuries of Latin American countries with US dollars coming from increased economic activity and especially from the big jump in the price of commodities. This has led most countries to run fiscal surpluses which then were used to increase the welfare of the citizens. But, in general, this positive economic wave has not been enough to effect a change in the Latin American economic and development model; this has been mainly due to political reasons and the short-sighted vision of many of the governments. The only exception may be Chile, which has set up a sovereign fund based overseas with the excess income coming from the high price of copper which will be invested in the long-term development of a new economic model. Brazil is currently attempting to do something similar. This raises the question about the model Latin Americans want for the growth and development of their region: do they want to continue relying on the exports of primary products? Or are they going to use this opportunity to add more value to the abundant resources in the region?

In this sense, a good option for Latin American countries may be deepening the economic integration in the region. It is clear that UNASUR needs Mexico and Mexico needs UNASUR, and it is also clear that they need to increase the trade between them. Some evidence of this seems to be appearing (see Table 6.2) but this recent trend needs to be sustained in the long term. To do this, Mexico is facing a dilemma: whether to strengthen links with its neighbours in the south, or to capitalise on its NAFTA membership. The former would give Latin America a much stronger weight in the world stage and at the same time better access to the growing middle-class markets in the south for Mexican companies. The latter would make Mexico a platform for Chinese companies to set up facilities to manufacture parts of their products in the country to then be re-exported to the United States or Canada. An example of this is the planned 'Dragon Mart', a US $2 billion complex funded by Chinese companies to create a manufacturing and logistics centre in Mexico to reach the North American markets which also includes 4,500 homes for Chinese expatriates and families (Xiong, 2011). The same idea of economic integration applies for Central American and the Caribbean countries; by working together they can negotiate better and overcome their small sizes.

On the other hand, a similar question on the future development model could be raised for the multilatinas. They have enjoyed a decade of growth fuelled by high commodity prices and low-cost capital, and as seen in Chapter 6 some of them are starting to go international. But this process is still far from being a strong trend. As discussed at the beginning of this chapter the future competition for markets will be in emerging economies, but what it is not clear yet is where multilatinas are placed for this battle.

8.4 Concluding remarks

After analysing what is going on between China and Latin America in the last five to seven years it is clear that Chinese companies are changing Latin America. But what it is not that clear is how Latin America is changing to deal with this. To decide what to do, Latin Americans need to recognise that Chinese firms are more than low-cost manufacturers; they have the economic muscle of the Chinese government, they have access to the financial markets and they also have a set of capabilities that are becoming stronger as they grow.

Another concern is the environment, especially as China is likely to continue investing in natural resources. As seen in Chapter 4, Chinese expect environmental issues to be regulated by authorities in each locality rather than by self-regulation, and also some Latin American governments may be tempted to prioritise the economic growth of the region over the protection of the environment. This combination is a dangerous one and it may lead to future problems. In the meantime, it does not seem that the environment is on Chinese companies' agenda.

Finally and more broadly, as it has been repeated throughout this book, the growing importance of emerging markets is affecting the dynamics of globalisation. In this context the relationship between China and Latin America is leading the process by opening a new South–South axis of trade, by attracting around 40% of the world's FDI, and by hosting companies that are becoming global players in their industries. This new axis is rivalling those of the Triad and it is becoming the emerging markets' axis.

Appendix 1
China's Policy Paper on Latin America and the Caribbean (Gov.cn, 2008)

The Chinese government launched its first ever policy paper on Latin America and the Caribbean region. The full text of the policy paper is as follows:

Foreword

The world today is undergoing major transformation and adjustment. Peace and development are the trend of the times. The move toward multi-polarity is irreversible and economic globalisation is gaining momentum. World peace and development are facing new opportunities as well as various challenges. It is in the fundamental interest of people of all countries and also their common aspiration to share development opportunities, jointly address challenges and promote the noble cause of peace and development of mankind.

As the largest developing country in the world, China is committed to the path of peaceful development and the win-win strategy of opening-up. It is ready to carry out friendly cooperation with all countries on the basis of the Five Principles of Peaceful Coexistence and build a harmonious world of durable peace and common prosperity.

Latin American and Caribbean countries are an important part of the developing world and a major force in the international arena. Under new circumstances, the development of relations between China and Latin American and Caribbean countries is faced with new opportunities. In issuing this policy paper on Latin America and the Caribbean, the Chinese Government aims to further clarify the goals of China's policy in this region, outline the guiding principles for future cooperation between the two sides in various fields and sustain the sound, steady and all-round growth of China's relations with Latin America and the Caribbean.

A1.1 The status and role of Latin America and the Caribbean

Latin America and the Caribbean have a long history, vast territory and abundant resources, and the region enjoys a good foundation for economic and social growth and huge development potential.

Countries in the region have been actively exploring development paths suited to their national conditions. They have maintained political stability and continued economic growth, and the life of the people is steadily improving. Latin American and Caribbean countries cherish a strong desire for self-development through unity and the commitment to promoting regional peace, stability and development. The region on the whole is growing in strength and its international influence is rising. Latin American and Caribbean countries have taken an active part in international affairs and contributed significantly to world peace and common development. They are playing an increasingly important role in regional and international affairs.

A1.2 China's relations with Latin America and the Caribbean

Though China and Latin America and the Caribbean are far from each other, the two peoples enjoy a time-honoured friendship. The two sides are at a similar stage of development and face the common task of achieving development. Both sides cherish the desire for greater mutual understanding and closer cooperation.

During the twenty years or so after the founding of New China in 1949, China and Latin America and the Caribbean mainly conducted people-to-people exchanges. In the 1970s and 1980s, China established diplomatic ties with most countries in the region. Friendly cooperation between the two sides in various fields registered momentous growth in the 1990s. Since the beginning of the twenty-first century, the two sides have enjoyed more frequent high-level exchanges, stronger political mutual trust and closer cooperation in economy, trade, science and technology, culture and education, and mutual support and close coordination in international affairs. New progress has been made in relations between the two sides in an all-round way at various levels and across a broad spectrum of areas.

Friendly cooperation between China and Latin America and the Caribbean serves the fundamental interest of the two peoples. Future growth of relationship between the two sides enjoys great potential and broad prospects, and will contribute more significantly to peace and development of mankind.

A1.3 China's policy on Latin America and the Caribbean

To enhance solidarity and cooperation with other developing countries is the cornerstone of China's independent foreign policy of peace. The Chinese Government views its relations with Latin America and the Caribbean from a strategic plane and seeks to build and develop a comprehensive and cooperative partnership featuring equality, mutual benefit and common development with Latin American and Caribbean countries. The goals of China's policy on Latin America and the Caribbean are:

- Promote mutual respect and mutual trust and expand common ground. Based on the Five Principles of Peaceful Coexistence, China and Latin America and the Caribbean will treat each other as equals and respect each other. They will strengthen dialogue and communication, enhance political mutual trust, expand strategic common ground, and continue to show understanding and support on issues involving each other's core interests and major concerns.
- Deepen cooperation and achieve win-win results. The two sides will leverage their respective strengths, tap the potential of cooperation, and seek to become each other's partner in economic cooperation and trade for mutual benefit and common development.
- Draw on each other's strengths to boost common progress and intensify exchanges. The two sides will carry out more cultural and people-to-people exchanges, learn from each other and jointly promote development and progress of human civilisation.
- The one China principle is the political basis for the establishment and development of relations between China and Latin American and Caribbean countries and regional organisations. The overwhelming majority of countries in the region are committed to the one China policy and the position of supporting China's reunification and not having official ties or contacts with Taiwan. The Chinese Government appreciates such a stance. China is ready to establish and develop state-to-state relations with all Latin American and Caribbean countries based on the one China principle.

A1.4 Strengthen China's comprehensive cooperation with Latin American and Caribbean Region

In the political field

(1) High-level exchanges

China wishes to maintain the momentum of close exchanges with leaders of Latin American and Caribbean countries to increase mutual understanding and trust, step up exchange of experience on governance and consolidate the political basis for the growth of relations with Latin American and Caribbean countries.

(2) Exchanges between legislatures

The National People's Congress of China wishes to strengthen friendly exchanges with parliaments of Latin American and Caribbean countries, the Latin American Parliament, the Mercosur Parliament, the Andean Parliament, etc. at multiple levels and through various channels on the basis of respecting each other, deepening mutual understanding and promoting cooperation so as to enrich and invigorate relations with Latin American and Caribbean countries.

(3) Exchanges between Political Parties

The Communist Party of China wishes to carry out friendly exchanges of various forms with political parties and organisations of Latin American and Caribbean countries on the basis of independence, full equality, mutual respect and non-interference in each other's internal affairs to learn from each other, increase mutual understanding and friendship, and strengthen mutual trust and cooperation.

(4) Consultation mechanisms

Relevant agencies of the Chinese Government wish to establish and improve the mechanisms of standing committee, high-level committee, high-level mixed committee, strategic dialogue, political consultation, mixed committee on economy and trade, consultation on economy and trade, high-level working group, business cooperation forum, cultural and education mixed committee, and science and technology committee with their counterparts in Latin America and the Caribbean to increase consultation and promote exchanges and cooperation.

(5) Cooperation in international affairs

The Chinese Government will continue to strengthen coordination and cooperation on international issues with Latin American and

Caribbean countries, and maintain regular consultation with them on major international and regional issues. The two sides will continue to support each other on such important issues as sovereignty and territorial integrity. China stands ready to work with Latin American and Caribbean countries to strengthen the role of the United Nations, make the international political and economic order more fair and equitable, promote democracy in international relations and uphold the legitimate rights and interests of developing countries. China supports a greater role of Latin American and Caribbean countries in international affairs.

(6) Local government exchanges

The Chinese side highly values exchanges at the local government level with countries in Latin America and the Caribbean. It supports the twinning of provinces/states or cities between China and Latin American and Caribbean countries, and exchanges and cooperation in business, science and technology, culture and other fields to increase mutual understanding and friendship. It attaches great importance to cooperation with Latin American and Caribbean countries in international local government organisations.

In the economic field

(1) Trade

The Chinese Government will continue to work with its Latin American and Caribbean counterparts in the spirit of equality and mutual benefit to expand and balance two-way trade and improve the trade structure to achieve common development. At the same time, it will work with these countries to properly settle trade frictions through consultation and cooperation. China will, on the basis of mutual benefit and win-win cooperation, give positive consideration to concluding free trade agreements with Latin American and Caribbean countries or regional integration organisations.

(2) Investment cooperation

The Chinese Government encourages and supports qualified Chinese companies with good reputation in investing in manufacturing, agriculture, forestry, fishing, energy, mineral resources, infrastructure, and service sector in Latin America and the Caribbean to promote the economic and social development of both sides. The Chinese Government will continue to welcome investment by Latin American and Caribbean businesses in China.

(3) Financial cooperation

The Chinese Government supports China's monetary and financial regulatory authorities and financial institutions in stepping up consultation and professional exchanges and cooperation on macroeconomic situation and economic and financial policies with their counterparts in Latin American and Caribbean countries. It encourages Chinese commercial banks to set up branches in Latin America and the Caribbean. It will push for the conclusion of banking regulatory cooperation agreements with Latin American and Caribbean countries as appropriate, and work with them to jointly combat money laundering and terrorist financing.

(4) Agricultural cooperation

The Chinese Government will promote exchanges and cooperation in agricultural science and technology with Latin American and Caribbean countries through holding agricultural technique training programs and dispatching technicians to the Latin American and Caribbean region. An information exchange mechanism will be established to discuss issues of common interest. Cooperation in flora and fauna inspection will be intensified and agricultural trade will be expanded to jointly uphold food security.

(5) Industrial cooperation

The Chinese side wishes to strengthen exchanges with Latin American and Caribbean countries in industry. It is desirable to establish and improve relevant cooperation mechanisms, share best practices in each other's industrialisation process, and promote and deepen practical cooperation.

(6) Infrastructure construction

The Chinese side will strengthen practical cooperation with Latin American and Caribbean countries in transport, information and communications, water conservancy and hydropower and other areas of infrastructure development, scale up project contracting in the region, and conduct mutually beneficial cooperation in various ways so as to contribute its share to further infrastructure development in the region.

(7) Resources and energy cooperation

The Chinese side wishes to expand and deepen mutually beneficial cooperation with Latin American and Caribbean countries in resources and energy within bilateral cooperation frameworks.

(8) Customs cooperation

The Chinese side wishes to strengthen exchanges and cooperation with Latin American and Caribbean countries on customs by increasing exchanges between customs officers of the two sides and promoting trade security and facilitation. Exchanges and consultation will be increased on issues of mutual concern, such as smuggling and business fraud. Negotiations aimed at concluding documents on mutual administrative assistance with customs authorities of relevant countries will be held in due course.

(9) Cooperation on quality inspection

The Chinese Government wishes to step up exchanges and cooperation with Latin American and Caribbean countries on quality inspection, technical barriers to trade (WTO/TBT) and sanitary and phytosanitary measures (WTO/SPS), and establish and improve consultation mechanisms on quality inspection to ensure product quality and food safety. The two sides will strengthen exchanges and consultation on issues of mutual interest such as product quality, food safety, and quarantine of entry animals and plants, leading to the signing of protocols on quarantine of entry products. They will also conduct active exchanges and cooperation on measurement and standardisation.

(10) Tourism cooperation

The Chinese side will expand tourism cooperation with Latin American and Caribbean countries to enhance mutual understanding and friendship between the two peoples. The Chinese side will make vigorous efforts to promote visits by Chinese tourist groups to Latin American and Caribbean countries. It also welcomes citizens of Latin American and Caribbean countries to visit China.

(11) Debt reduction and cancellation

The Chinese Government will, based on its consistent policy on debt reduction and cancellation, discuss with relevant Latin American and Caribbean countries ways to relieve their debts as China's ability permits. The Chinese Government will also continue to call upon the international community, developed countries in particular, to take more concrete steps to reduce and cancel debts owed by Latin American and Caribbean countries.

(12) Economic and technical assistance

The Chinese Government will, according to its financial capability and level of economic and social development, continue to provide economic and technical assistance to relevant Latin American and Caribbean countries without attaching any political conditions. The Chinese Government will work within its ability and gradually increase its assistance to Latin American and Caribbean countries to meet their needs.

(13) Multilateral cooperation

The Chinese Government is ready to strengthen consultation and coordination with Latin American and Caribbean countries in multilateral trade and financial institutions and regimes, with a view to promoting South–South cooperation, bringing about a more just and equitable multilateral trading regime and ensuring a bigger say and greater role in decision-making for developing countries in international trade and financial affairs.

(14) Chamber-of-commerce cooperation

The Chinese side will deepen its cooperation with chambers of commerce of Latin America and the Caribbean and push forward exchanges between business communities of the two sides through the China–Latin America Entrepreneur Summit, China-Caribbean Entrepreneurs Meeting and other mechanisms, in an effort to achieve win-win results.

In the cultural and social aspects

(1) Cultural and sports exchanges

The Chinese Government will work actively to follow up on cultural cooperation agreements and relevant implementation programs signed with Latin American and Caribbean countries, maintain regular exchange of visits between cultural authorities of the two sides, and strengthen interaction and cooperation between cultural and art institutions and professionals of the two sides. To meet the needs for cultural exchange and market demand, the two sides will provide guidance for and push forward a variety of cultural exchange programs among various communities of the two sides.

The Chinese side will keep the momentum of exchanges between the sports authorities and national Olympic committees, and encourage direct contacts between sports associations of the two sides. Guidance and encouragement will also be given to bilateral sports exchanges in various forms.

(2) Cooperation in science, technology and education

The Chinese side is ready to enhance scientific and technological exchanges with Latin American and Caribbean countries through the mixed committee on bilateral science and technology cooperation and high-level coordinating mechanism. The Chinese side will also strengthen cooperation with Latin America and the Caribbean in aeronautics and astronautics, bio-fuel, resources and environment technology, marine technology and other areas of shared interest. The Chinese side will promote wider application of Chinese technologies on energy-conservation, digital medical treatment, small hydropower and other results of scientific research and advanced applied techniques in Latin America and the Caribbean. The Chinese side will provide Latin American and Caribbean countries with technical training, services and demonstration, and step up cooperation and exchanges on the educational front with Latin American and Caribbean countries through bilateral and multilateral cooperation mechanisms. The Chinese side will work for the conclusion of the agreement on mutual recognition of diplomas and academic degrees, and increase the number of Chinese government scholarships for Latin American and Caribbean countries.

(3) Cooperation in medical and health care

The Chinese Government will vigorously promote exchanges and cooperation in the medical and health care sector with Latin American and Caribbean countries, and share experience and carry out cooperation in such areas as disease control, response to public health emergencies, and control of HIV/AIDS and bird flu. The Chinese Government will continue to send medical contingents equipped with necessary medicines and medical equipments to relevant countries to help improve local medical facilities and train local medical professionals.

(4) Consular cooperation and personnel exchanges

The Chinese Government will develop and deepen consular relations with Latin American and Caribbean countries, and strengthen and expand exchanges and cooperation between the consular departments of the two sides. The Chinese Government will carry out bilateral or multilateral friendly discussions with Latin American and Caribbean countries on consular issues of shared interest to address each other's concerns through the establishment of a consular consultation mechanism. The Chinese Government will take effective measures to promote and safeguard regular personnel exchanges between the two sides, facilitate normal trade, investment and business activities and uphold the lawful rights and interests of people of the two sides.

(5) Media cooperation

The Chinese Government encourages and actively promotes exchanges and cooperation between the media of the two sides at multiple levels and in various forms to increase mutual understanding and ensure comprehensive and unbiased reports of each other. It will work to increase communication and cooperation between government information departments of the two sides and provide convenience for media interaction and cooperation between the two sides.

(6) People-to-people exchanges

The Chinese Government encourages exchanges between non-governmental organisations and academic institutions of the two sides and gives full play to the role of the mechanism for people-to-people friendly interaction in advancing friendly relations between China and Latin American and Caribbean countries. It will strengthen interaction with youth organisations and institutions of Latin American and Caribbean countries, and deepen friendly cooperation with women's organisations at the national, regional and non-governmental levels in Latin American and Caribbean countries, so as to build up mutual understanding and mutual trust and work together for gender equality and the advancement of women.

(7) Cooperation in environmental protection

The Chinese side will strengthen exchanges with Latin American and Caribbean countries in laws, regulations and policies related to environmental protection and promote cooperation in personnel training, education and capacity building in the fields of biodiversity conservation, as well as prevention and treatment of pollution and desertification.

(8) Cooperation in combating climate change

The Chinese Government highly values its cooperation with Latin American and Caribbean countries in combating climate change and is ready to develop and consolidate bilateral cooperation under the United Nations Framework Convention on Climate Change and other relevant mechanisms. It will actively promote consultation and communication between the two sides on combating climate change and cooperation in related projects.

(9) Cooperation in human resources and social security

The Chinese side will strengthen exchanges and cooperation with Latin American and Caribbean countries in employment promotion, establishment of good labour relations, improvement of the social security system, human resources development and reform of the civil service system. It will, through the signing and implementation of memoranda of understanding on bilateral cooperation, deepen and expand bilateral exchanges in social aspects, and enhance coordination and cooperation between the two sides in international organisations such as the International Labour Organization.

(10) Disaster reduction, disaster relief and humanitarian assistance

The Chinese Government will enhance information sharing, experience exchanges and technological cooperation in disaster reduction and relief with Latin American and Caribbean countries and facilitate the establishment of regular bilateral and multilateral meeting mechanisms between relevant departments of the two sides. It will continue to respond positively to the need for urgent humanitarian assistance of Latin American and Caribbean countries. It will encourage non-governmental organisations such as the Red Cross Society of China to conduct exchanges and cooperation with relevant Latin American and Caribbean organisations in this regard.

(11) Cooperation in poverty alleviation

The Chinese Government will strengthen exchanges and cooperation with Latin American and Caribbean countries in reducing poverty and narrowing the gap between the rich and the poor, and will encourage poverty alleviation institutions of the two sides to establish broad cooperative relations to share information and conduct joint research. More training programs designed for poverty alleviation personnel in Latin American and Caribbean countries will be launched, while more interaction on poverty reduction with interstate or regional organisations in Latin America and the Caribbean will be strengthened. The two sides will also exchange visits and mutual participation in conferences and for poverty alleviation held by the other side.

On peace, security and judicial affairs

(1) Military exchanges and cooperation

The Chinese side will actively carry out military exchanges and defence dialogue and cooperation with Latin American and Caribbean countries. Mutual visits by defence and military officials of the two sides as well as personnel exchanges will be enhanced. Professional exchanges in military training, personnel training and peacekeeping will be deepened. Practical cooperation in the non-traditional security field will be expanded. The Chinese side will, as its ability permits, continue to provide assistance for the development of the army in Latin American and Caribbean countries.

(2) Cooperation in judicial and police affairs

The Chinese side will steadily expand its cooperation with Latin American and Caribbean countries in judicial affairs, judicial assistance in criminal and civil matters and extradition in particular. Cooperation in information sharing, penalty enforcement and legal services will be strengthened. Concerted efforts in law enforcement involving the interior and police departments of relevant countries will be stepped up to jointly combat transnational organised crimes including drug crimes and economic crimes. Intelligence and technological exchanges will be strengthened, with bilateral and multilateral exchange mechanisms put in place, so as to share information on illegal immigration and improve the capacity for its prevention.

(3) Non-traditional security issues

The Chinese Government will further its exchanges and cooperation with Latin American and Caribbean countries on non-traditional security issues by increasing information sharing and personnel exchanges and explore effective ways to deepen cooperation on non-traditional security issues such as combating terrorism, so as to jointly improve the capacity to respond to non-traditional security threats.

A1.5 China's relations with Latin American and Caribbean regional organisations

The Chinese Government appreciates the important role of Latin American and Caribbean regional and sub-regional organisations in safeguarding peace and stability in the region, and promoting regional solidarity, development and integration. It supports these organisations in exerting their influence in regional and international affairs. The Chinese side will continue to strengthen communication, consultation and cooperation with relevant organisations in various fields.

Appendix 2
Latibex

A2.1 What is Latibex?[1]

Latibex is the only international market for Latin American securities. The market's creation, in December 1999, was approved by the Spanish government and it is regulated by the Spanish Securities Market Law.

Latibex is an ideal way to channel European investment efficiently towards Latin America. European investors can buy and sell shares and securities in leading Latin American companies through a single market, with a single operating system for trading and settlement and a single currency, the euro. The market is based on the trading and settlement platform of the Spanish stock market in such a way that the Latin American securities listed on Latibex are traded and settled like any other Spanish security.

Meanwhile, Latibex gives Latin American companies easy and efficient access to the European capital market. In short, it brings European investors close to one of the world's most economically attractive regions, streamlining the operational and legal complexity and reducing risks. And this is all achieved in an environment of considerable information transparency.

The Bolsa de Madrid has also consolidated Latibex's innovative technical and functional organisation. The co-ordination agreements between Latibex and Latin American stock markets make for shared and integrated management which, as well as spurring development of the market, promotes its advantages more widely.

A2.2 Main features of Latibex

- Market authorised by the Spanish government.
- Trading and settlement platform in Europe of the main Latin American companies.
- Currency: trading in euros.
- Trading: the SIBE, Spanish electronic trading system.
- Settlement: D+3 through book entries.

- Connected to the market of origin under agreements of Iberclear with Latin American custodians or a link entity.
- Brokers: all members of the Spanish stock market. Members of Latin American markets can also operate.
- Specialist brokers: they provide a purchase and sale price at all times, linked to a certain trading volume in order to meet the requirements of any investor.

A2.3 Indices[2]

- FTSE Latibex All Share, which covers all the companies traded on Latibex.
- FTSE Latibex Top, which covers the 15 most liquid securities traded on Latibex.
- FTSE Latibex Brasil, which covers the most liquid securities from Brazil traded on Latibex.

Table A2.1 Latibex's issuing companies and shares

Name	Share Code	ISIN Code	T.U.
ALFA, S.A.B. DE C.V.			
ALFA,CLASE I SERIE A	XALFA	MXP000511016	10
AMERICA MOVIL, S.A.B. DE C.V.			
AMERICA MOVIL SERIE L	XAMXL	MXP001691213	20
BANCO BRADESCO S.A.			
BANCO BRADESCO PREF.	XBBDC	BRBBDCACNPR8	1
BANCO DE CHILE			
BANCO DE CHILE	XBCH	CLP0939W1081	600
BANCO SANTANDER RIO, S.A.			
BANCO SANTANDER RIO ORD. B	XBRSB	ARBRIO010194	1
BBVA BANCO FRANCES,S.A.			
BBVA BANCO FRANCES ORDINARIAS	XBFR	ARP125991090	1
BRADESPAR,S.A.			
BRADESPAR PREFERENTES	XBRPP	BRBRAPACNPR2	1
BRADESPAR ORDINARIAS	XBRPO	BRBRAPACNOR5	1
BRASKEM,S.A.			
BRASKEM PREFERENTES CLASE A	XBRK	BRBRKMACNPA4	1
CENTRAIS ELE. BRASILEIRA S.A. ELETROBRAS			
ELETROBRAS PREF.SERIE B	XELTB	BRELETACNPB7	1
ELETROBRAS ORDINARIAS	XELTO	BRELETACNOR6	1

Continued

Table A2.1 Continued

Name	Share Code	ISIN Code	T.C.
COM.ENERGETICA DE MINAS GER AIS-CEMIG			
CIA.ENERG.DE MINAS GERAIS PREF.	XCMIG	BRCMIGACNPR3	1
COMPANHIA PARANAENSE DE ENERGIA-COPEL B			
COPEL PREF.B	XCOP	BRCPLEACNPB9	1
CORPORACION GEO, S.A.B. DE C.V.			
GEO ORDINARIAS B	XGEO	MXP3142C1177	1
EMPRESA NACIONAL DE ELECTRICIDAD (CHILE)			
ENDESA CHILE	XEOC	CLP3710M1090	30
ENERSIS,S.A.			
ENERSIS	XENI	CLP371861061	50
GERDAU,S.A.			
GERDAU PREF.	XGGB	BRGGBRACNPR8	1
GRUPO DE INVERSIONES SURAMERICANA			
GRUPO DE INVERSIONES SURAMERICANA	XGSUR	COT13PA00011	1
GRUPO ELEKTRA, S.A. DE C. V.			
GRUPO ELEKTRA	XEKT	MX01EL000003	1
GRUPO FINANCIERO BANORTE S.A.B. DE C.V			
GRUPO FINANCIERO BANORTE	XNOR	MXP370711014	10
GRUPO MODELO, S.A.B. DE C.V.			
GRUPO MODELO CLASE C	XGMD	MXP4833F1044	10
NAFINSA, NACIONAL FINANCIERA NSC			
ISHARES NAFTRAC MEXICO	XNAFT	MX1BNA060006	10
NET SERVICOS DE COMUNICACAO, S.A.			
NET SERVIÇOS DE COMUNICAÇAO PREF.	XNET	BRNETCACNPR3	1
PETROLEO BRASILEIRO,S.A. (PETROBRAS)			
PETROLEO BRASILEIRO(PETROBRAS) O.	XPBR	BRPETRACNOR9	1
PETROLEO BRASILEIRO(PETROBRAS) P.	XPBRA	BRPETRACNPR6	1
SARE HOLDING, S.A.B, DE C.V.			
SARE HOLDING B	XSARE	MX01SA030007	10
SUZANO BAHIA SUL PAPEL E CELULOSE, S.A.			

Continued

Table A2.1 Continued

Name	Share Code	ISIN Code	T.U.
SUZANO BAHIA PREFERENTES-A	XSUZB	BRSUZBACNPA3	1
TELEFONOS DE MEXICO,S.A.B. DE C.V.			
TELEFONOS DE MEXICO, SERIE L	XTMXL	MXP904131325	20
TV AZTECA, S.A. DE C.V.			
TV AZTECA	XTZA	MXP740471117	10
USINAS SIDERURGICAS DE MINAS GERAIS,S.A.			
USIMINAS PREF. SERIE A	XUSI	BRUSIMACNPA6	1
USIMINAS ORDINARIAS	XUSIO	BRUSIMACNOR3	1
VALE, S.A.			
VALE ORDINARIAS	XVALO	BRVALEACNOR0	1
VALE PREFERENTES	XVALP	BRVALEACNPA3	1
VOLCAN, COMPAñIA MINERA S.A.A.			
VOLCAN COMPAÑIA MINERA CLASE B	XVOLB	PEP648014202	10

Appendix 3
American Depository Receipts

A3.1 ADRs[1]

Historically, American Depositary Receipts (ADRs) were the first type of depositary receipt to evolve. They were introduced in 1927 in response to a law passed in Britain, which prohibited British companies from registering shares overseas without a British-based transfer agent. UK shares were not allowed physically to leave the UK, and so, to accommodate US investor demand, a US instrument had to be created: this was called an American Depositary Receipt. ADRs assumed their present form in 1955, when the Securities and Exchange Commission (SEC) established its Form S-12 for registering all depositary receipt programs. Form S-12 was later replaced by Form F-6, which is still in use today.

ADRs are US dollar denominated negotiable instruments issued in the US by a depositary bank (e.g., Deutsche Bank), representing ownership in non-US securities, usually referred to as the underlying ordinary shares. ADRs enable US investors to acquire and trade non-US securities denominated in US dollars without concern for the differing settlement timetables and the problems typically associated with overseas markets. They also provide non-US companies with access to the US capital markets, the largest domestic investor base in the world.

A3.2 Capital raising and non-capital raising ADRs

There are several types of ADR, each of which involves a different level of disclosure of information and compliance with the regulations of the SEC. But perhaps the most important distinction for issuers of ADRs is that some structures allow the company to raise capital in the United States, while others simply provide a mechanism which makes it easy for US investors to buy and trade existing shares.

A3.3 Global Depositary Receipts (GDRs)/European Depositary Receipts (EDRs)

In the last few years, the depositary receipt concept has developed considerably. Issuers in a variety of countries have realised that there are advantages in making their stock available in a form convenient not only to US investors but also, or alternatively, to investors in the Euromarkets or elsewhere. This has prompted the development of European Depositary Receipts (EDRs) and Global Depositary Receipts (GDRs).

The EDR accesses the Euromarkets but not the US market. It settles and trades through the Euromarket clearing systems, Euroclear and Clearstream, and it may be listed on a European Stock Exchange, normally London or Luxembourg.

A GDR will access two or more markets, usually the Euromarkets (like an EDR) and the US (like an ADR). GDRs are often launched for capital raising purposes, so the US element is generally either a Rule 144(a) ADR or a Level III ADR, depending on whether the issuer aims to tap the private placement or public US markets.

EDRs and GDRs are generally denominated in US dollars, but they may be denominated in any currency. They represent the underlying shares in exactly the same way as ADRs, and they make it possible for foreign investors to trade in the issuing company's stock without the problems associated with custody and settlement in foreign markets.

A3.4 Buying and Selling DRs

If an investor wishes to purchase shares in a foreign company, he can either buy the foreign shares in the local market through a broker in that country or, providing the foreign company in question has a DR program, the investor can request his broker to buy DRs. The broker may either purchase existing DRs or, if none are available, he may arrange for a depositary bank (e.g., Deutsche Bank) to issue new ones.

The process for issuing new DRs is very simple. The investor's broker contacts a broker in the issuing company's home market and acquires shares in that company. These shares are then deposited with the depositary bank's local custodian. Upon confirmation that the custodian has received the shares, the depositary issues the requisite number of DRs to the investor via the broker.

In some exceptional cases there may be restrictions on the issuance of new DRs under existing programs (e.g., Indian GDR programs) because of local regulations.

DRs can be sold in DR form, in which case they trade and settle like other US or Euro securities. They can also, however, be cancelled. In this case the broker acting on behalf of the owner of the DRs will request the depositary bank to cancel the DRs and release the underlying shares to a domestic broker in the issuing company's home market. The domestic broker will then sell the shares locally and the proceeds will be remitted to the investor who cancelled those DRs.

- DRs certify that a stated number of underlying shares have been deposited with the depositary's custodian in the foreign country.
- DR holders are entitled to all the dividends payable on the underlying foreign shares and, furthermore, to have these paid in the currency in which the DRs are denominated – usually US dollars.
- The DRs may be bought or sold through investors' own brokers, and they clear and settle through the Depository Trust Company (DTC) for ADRs, through Euroclear and Clearstream for EDRs and through all three (and possibly other clearing systems) in the case of GDRs, depending on which markets they access.

Shareholder information such as annual reports, notices of general meetings and corporate actions, and official news releases are provided by the issuer to the depositary and to the receipt holders, either directly or through the local custodian.

The investor is thus spared the costs and difficulties often encountered when direct investment is made in local markets, where currency, settlement and linguistic problems may be compounded by an excessive number of intermediaries.

A3.5 Why do investors buy DRs?

US investors have become increasingly interested in overseas markets as a result of their higher yields compared to the US equity market over recent years.

International investors are also eager to diversify their portfolios, both geographically and by industry sector, in order to increase their returns while spreading their risk. They have long been active in the debt markets, as evidenced by the vast size of the Euromarkets, and sophisticated international clearing systems have been developed to handle Euro instruments. Until recently, however, cross-border equity investments have involved all the currency, settlement and linguistic problems which occur when dealing with overseas equity markets.

Building on the concept of the ADR, investment banks developed the EDR/GDR to solve these problems for international investors.

Some of the factors contributing to the appeal of DRs to international investors:

- They offer investors a convenient means of holding foreign shares.
- They simplify the trading and settlement of foreign equities. DRs trade and settle just like US or Euro securities.
- They offer lower trading and custody costs when compared with shares bought directly in the foreign market.
- Many US bank and pension fund portfolios may be prohibited by their charters from purchasing foreign securities. ADRs, however, are recognised as US domestic securities.
- ADRs, and normally GDRs too, are denominated in US dollars. Dividend payments on the underlying shares are converted into US dollars by the depositary bank. These features minimise foreign exchange problems for international and US investors.

A3.6 Why do companies launch DR programs?

ADRs

ADR programs are becoming ever more attractive to non-US corporations as the most effective means of entering the important US market. Furthermore, certain types of ADR programs permit capital raising in the United States, and the amount of new capital raised through ADRs has risen, from US $2.5 billion in 1990 to more than US $27.7 billion in 2000. ADRs have also taken on increasing importance in cross-border merger and acquisition activity.

Advantages to a non-US corporation of initiating an ADR program:

- An ADR program provides a simple means of diversifying a company's shareholder base and accessing the important US market.
- It may increase the liquidity of the underlying shares of the issuer.
- ADRs can be used as an equity financing tool in both M&A transactions and ESOPs (Employee Stock Ownership Plans) for US subsidiaries.
- An ADR program helps to increase a non-US company's visibility and name recognition in the important US investor community.

- A company may raise capital in the US market through some types of ADR program.

EDRs/GDRs

The advantages of an EDR/GDR program are similar to those of an ADR program. An EDR program gives access to the vast pool of international capital, while a GDR combines this with access to the domestic US market.

This allows capital raising on a scale which could be difficult in some domestic markets, and in the case of an EDR, it avoids all the US SEC reporting and registration requirements associated with ADRs.

Advantages to a non-US corporation initiating an EDR/GDR program:

- A DR program provides a simple means of diversifying the company's shareholder base and of tapping the global capital markets.
- It allows capital raising on a scale which might prove impossible in the local market.
- It increases the issuer's visibility and name recognition in the international markets, which may enhance knowledge of its products and ease the path of future capital raising exercises.

A3.7 A useful structuring tool

While DRs are generally used to make equity more widely available or to raise capital outside the issuer's domestic market, they can also be used as part of many other financing structures. The concept of a receipt trading in one market, which represents an instrument held in custody in a different market, can be adapted to a wide variety of transactions.

Appendix 4
Chile–China Free Trade Agreement

A4.1 China[1]

With 1.3 billion inhabitants and a sustained economic growth of between 8% and 10% in the last decade, China plays today an increasingly gravitating role in global politics and economy. For many people, the phenomenon led by this country is considered to be a second industrial revolution.

The current growth rates of China find their origin in the program of reforms and economic opening conducted in China during the late '70s and early '80s decade, along with Chinese entry into the World Trade Organization (WTO) in 2001.

The explosive growth of the Chinese GDP over 8.5% in the last years (it has increased threefold during the last decade) has also turned it into a great consumer of energy and raw materials which has to seek such resources or supplies to be provided by other regions.

A4.2 Free trade agreement between China and Chile

Chile is the first non-Asian country that negotiated an FTA with China. With 1.3 billion inhabitants, it represents a very important potential market for the exporting of Chilean products; besides, it strengthens the presence of our country in Asia and serves as a bridge between such a dynamic zone and South America.

The accelerated and sustained growth of its GDP and their commercial exchanges, together with deep economic reforms that have been implemented which made it join the WTO, as well as the searching for bilateral agreements, have allowed this Asian nation to become the most dynamic actor in the worldwide economy.

A4.3 Negotiation process

In June of the 2002, the PRC proposed that Chile start negotiations for a Free Trade Agreement.

On 18 November 2004, after a feasibility study, in the framework of the bilateral activities of APEC Summit 2004, the president of Chile and the president of the People's Republic of China announced the beginning of negotiations for a future FTA.

The first round of negotiations was carried out in Beijing, from January 25 to 27, 2005, and the Commercial Negotiations Committee was established.

The second round of negotiations took place in Santiago, Chile, from April 27 to 29.

The third round of negotiations was held from June 28 to 30, in the city of Wuxi, China.

The fourth round of negotiations took place in Santiago between 12 and 16 of September.

The fifth and last round of negotiations was held between October 24 and 28, in Beijing, China. The meeting was concluded with the presence of the Minister of Foreign Affairs of Chile, Mr. Ignacio Walker, and the Minister of Commerce of China, Bo Xilai. Later on, during the 2005 APEC Summit carried out in Korea, they both signed the Agreement on 18 November 2005.

The Agreement began in Chile on 1 October 2006.

A4.4 Matters covered by the FTA

The final text of the agreement considers chapters on the following matters: institutional and administrative proceedings, market access, trade remedies, rules of origin, sanitary and phytosanitary measures, technical barriers to trade, dispute settlement and cooperation. A memorandum of understanding between the corresponding labour and social security authorities, and an agreement on environmental cooperation were also signed with the FTA.

A4.5 Tariff reduction program

A consensus was reached for the immediate reduction of tariffs on 92% of Chilean exports to China, applicable the first day in which the agreement becomes effective. For China, this percentage amounts to 50% of its current trade. The agreement also considers tariff reductions after 1, 5, and 10 years for Chilean products accessing China, and 5 and 10 years for Chinese exports to Chile. Product exclusions for 1% of Chilean exports and 3% of Chinese shipments to our country were also agreed upon.

Full text of the agreement can be found in:
http://www.direcon.cl/documentos/China2/tlc_chile_china_ing_junio_2006.pdf

A4.6 China–Chile FTA on service trade implemented (MOFCOM, 2010a)

The Supplementary Agreement on Service Trade to the Free Trade Agreement between the Government of the People's Republic of China and the Government of the Republic of Chile (China–Chile FTA on Service Trade) implemented on August 1, 2010.

China and Chile signed the Supplementary Agreement on April 13, 2008. According to the agreement, China's 23 sectors and subsectors, including service in the sector of computer, management and consulting, real estate, mining, environment, sports and air transport, and Chile's 37 sectors and subsectors, including service in the sector of legal service, construction and architecture, engineering, computer, R&D, real estate, advertisement, management and consulting, mining, manufacturing, leasing, distribution, education, environment, tourism, sports and air transport will further be opened up to each other under the WTO commitments.

The implementation of the agreement will further open up their own services market to each other, increase complementary advantages and promote international competitiveness, and help improve the investment environments, create business opportunities, reduce trading costs and bring more benefits to the enterprises and people of the two countries. It will help boost an all-around cooperation in all sectors between the two countries, broaden the cooperative areas and improve cooperation level for developing a comprehensive cooperative partnership.

China and Chile have maintained a sound and stable bilateral relationship since the establishment of diplomatic relations in 1970. On November 18, 2005, witnessed by Chinese President Hu Jintao and Former Chilean President Ricardo Lagos, the two sides signed China–Chile FTA (Mainly on Trade in Goods) which was effective on October 1, 2006.

Appendix 5
China and Peru Signed Free Trade Agreement

Witnessed by Chinese Vice President Xi Jinping and Peruvian Vice President Luis Giampietri Rojas, Yi Xiaozhun, Vice Minister of Commerce, and Mercedes Araoz Fernandez, Peruvian Minister of Trade and Tourism, signed, on behalf of their own government, China–Peru Free Trade Agreement (FTA) in the Great Hall of the People on April 28 China–Peru FTA, the first package FTA China signed with a country in Latin American, is a new landmark in bilateral ties.[1]

The China–Peru FTA features wide coverage and a high degree of openness. Over 90% of trade in goods between China and Peru will enjoy zero tariff on a stage-by-stage basis. Trade in goods covers China's products from light industry, electronics, home appliances, machinery, automobile, chemicals, vegetables, fruits and Peru's fish powder, minerals, fruits and fish products. Trade in services, both countries pledge to further open up their service sectors based on their respective commitments to WTO. In terms of investment, each side will give Post-Establishment National Treatment, MFN and Fair and Equitable Treatment to investors from the other side, and encourage and provide facilitation to investment. The two countries also reached agreements on such issues as intellectual property, trade relief, rules of origin, customs procedures, TBT and SPS, etc. More information can be found at 'China Free Trade Area Service' (fta.mofcom.gov.cn).

China and Peru commenced FTA negotiations on 7 September 2007, when Chinese President Hu Jintao and Peruvian President Garcia attended the APEC informal leadership meeting in Sydney, and announced jointly to commence the negotiation. Eight rounds of negotiation and one working group meeting were held before 19 November 2008 when President Hu Jintao was on a state visit to Peru and announced jointly with Peruvian President Garcia that China–Peru FTA negotiations had concluded successfully. China and Peru are strongly complementary in economy, and bilateral relations developed rapidly in recent years. At present, China is Peru's second largest trading partner, while Peru is China's seventh largest trading partner in Latin America. According to statistics from Chinese customs, bilateral trade in 2008 reached US $7.5 billion, up 24% compared with the previous year, among which China's exports are US $2.8 billion and imports are US $4.7 billion.

To date, China has signed FTA with ASEAN, Chile, Pakistan, New Zealand, Singapore and Peru, and it is negotiating FTA with Australia, the Gulf Cooperation Council (including six countries of Saudi Arabia, Kuwait, UAE, Oman, Qatar and Bahrain), Iceland, Norway, Costa Rica and the Southern African Customs Union.

Full text of the agreement can be found in:

http://www.mincetur.gob.pe/newweb/portals/0/comercio/tlc_china/textos_pagina/Ingles/TLC_Peru_China_Texto_completo_ingles.pdf

Appendix 6
China Signed Free Trade Agreement with Costa Rica (*People's Daily Online*, 2010)

China's commerce minister Chen Deming and his Costa Rican counterpart Marco Ruiz signed the China–Costa Rica Free Trade Agreement in Beijing on April 8. Both parties agreed that they will strive to implement the agreement in late 2010 after regulatory approval.

According to an official from the international division under the Ministry of Commerce, talks between China and Costa Rica were efficient as they only lasted one year and one month. Reporters learned that this is the first time China has signed a free trade package with a Central American country. So far, China has reached free trade deals with ASEAN member countries, Chile, Pakistan, New Zealand, Singapore, Peru and Costa Rica.

As for the trade of goods, at least 90% of the goods from both sides will gradually enjoy zero tariff access to each other's markets. The goods which will benefit from tariff reductions mainly include China's textile raw materials and products, light industrial products, machines, electrical equipment, vegetables, fruits, automobiles, chemical products, raw fur, leather products, as well as Costa Rica's coffee, beef, pork, pineapple juice, frozen orange juice, jams, fish meals, mineral products and rawhide.

As for service trade, Costa Rica will further open 45 service sectors to China, and China will further open 7 service sectors to Costa Rica, which is based on the WTO commitments of both sides. Meanwhile, the two sides have achieved broad consensus on rules of origin, customs procedures, technical barriers, sanitary and phytosanitary regulations, trade remedies and others.

Costa Rica is now an important Central American trading partner of China's and China is Costa Rica's second largest trading partner, only after the United States. According to statistics from China Customs, the China–Costa Rica bilateral trade volume reached nearly US $2.9 billion in 2008, 32 times more than in 2001. Although most major economies in the world fell into recession in terms of foreign trade in 2009, the China–Costa Rica bilateral trade volume rose to nearly US $3.2 billion in that year, up more than 10% compared to 2008. Moreover, China's imports from Costa Rica reached almost US $2.7 billion in 2009, up nearly 17% over 2008.

Full text of the agreement can be found in:
http://fta.mofcom.gov.cn/gesidalijia/xieyi/xieyi_en.rar

Notes

1 Introduction

1. Quoted in Dyer, Pilling and Henny, 2011.

2 Emerging Markets: The Markets of the Future

1. Quoted in McGregor, 2011.
2. www.g20.org
3. Quoted in *The Economist*, 2008.
4. The categorisation is based on four criteria: market and regulatory environment, custody and settlement, dealing landscape, derivatives.
5. 'FTSE Emerging Market indices are a segment of the overall FTSE Global Equity Index Series (GEIS), and contribute to the overall GEIS market coverage of 98% of the world's total investable market capitalisation, cover 48 countries and comprise over 7000 large, mid and small cap stocks. Our emerging market indices cover the same 48 countries and consist of approximately 1700 large, mid and small cap stocks. FTSE has divided the emerging markets into advanced emerging and secondary emerging markets for greater granularity and to provide a transparent system on the monitoring of emerging market criteria through a country review process. The FTSE All-World Index Series is the large/mid cap aggregate of 2,700 stocks from the FTSE Global Equity Index Series. It covers 90–95% of the investable market capitalisation' (FTSE, 2011).
6. Quoted in Hughes, 2011.
7. Hong Kong, China; Malaysia; Republic of Korea; Singapore; Separate Customs Territory of Taiwan, Penghu, Kinmen and Matsu (Taipei, Chinese), and Thailand (WTO, 2006).
8. All Latin American countries were colonised by Spain, their populations speak Spanish, and they are Roman Catholics, with the exception of Brazil, which was colonised by Portugal and their population speaks Portuguese.
9. Japan, North America and Western Europe (Omae, 1985).

3 China–Latin America: The Emerging Markets' Axis

1. Santiso, 2006a, p. 96.
2. www.mercosur.int
3. www.comunidadandina.org
4. www.caricom.org
5. www.ustr.gov/trade-agreements/free-trade-agreements/cafta-dr-dominican-republic-central-america-fta
6. www.pptunasur.com
7. Official site: www.argentina.gov.ar

8. Official site: www.brasil.gov.br
9. Official site: www.gob.cl
10. Official site: www.presidencia.gov.co
11. Official site: www.casapres.go.cr
12. Official site: www.presidencia.gov.ec
13. Official site: www.gob.mx
14. Official site: www.peru.gob.pe
15. Official site: www.presidencia.gob.ve
16. Official site: www.gov.cn
17. http://ec.europa.eu/agriculture/publi/capexplained/cap_en.pdf

5 Chinese Dragons Disembarking in Latin America

1. Williamson and Yin, 2009, p. 78.
2. This chapter is based on Fornes, 2011; Fornes and Butt-Philip, 2008; Fornes and Butt-Philip, 2009, 2011a, 2011b.
3. This section is based on Cardoza and Fornes, 2009; Cardoza and Fornes, 2011; Fornes and Cardoza, 2010.
4. This section is based on Fornes and Butt-Philip, 2011b.
5. In fact, it has been suggested that China is using trade and investment agreements, among other things, to ensure recognition of its market status economy by the counterpart countries (ECLAC, 2005, 2007). So far, most of the states that have recognised China as a market status economy are developing countries; in addition, ECLAC (2007) stated that many of these agreements do not include sensitive products or sectors such as the protection of intellectual property, the liberalisation of sectors or issues related to labour or the environment (the latter may explain why China is pursuing agreements with developing countries (ECLAC, 2007), as it will probably find a limited reception with industrialised countries if, for example, these sensitive areas were not included in the agreements).
6. Europe has been a major foreign investor in Latin America since the beginning of the twentieth century, with the UK being the largest European investor for most of the first 90 years. Spain started to become a relevant player 'in 1991 when Telefónica won the bid for the privatisation of Entel in Argentina and reached a peak (in terms of the amount of investment) in 1999 when Repsol acquired YPF in Argentina for around €15 billion' (Fornes and Cardoza, 2007). After 1997, Latin America received around 60% of Spanish foreign investments (as an annual average), which positioned Latin America as the first destination for Spanish companies, and Spain as the second largest international investor in the region after the United States (Fornes, 2009; Fornes and Butt-Philip, 2009; Fornes and Cardoza, 2007).

6 Multilatinas and the China Challenge

1. Naim, 2011.
2. Colombia is considered investment grade by S&P only, Moody's and Fitch Ratings consider it investment-grade for long term in local currency.
3. Characteristics taken from Aguiar et al., 2009, p. 9.

8 Conclusions

1. Wolf, 2011.

Appendix 2

1. Latibex, 2011.
2. The indices are drawn up in conjunction with the FTSE, the company responsible for the indices of the Financial Times Group. Transparent information: the listed companies provide the market with the same information they supply to the regulatory entities of their markets of origin.

Appendix 3

1. Deutsche Bank, 2011a.

Appendix 4

1. National Customs Service Gobierno de Chile, 2011.

Appendix 5

1. MOFCOM, 2009b.

References

Agence France Presse. 2009. Ecuador leader: negotiating with China like pulling teeth. *Agence France Presse*. 5/12/2009.

Aguiar, M., Becerra, J., de Juan, J., León, E., Nieponice, G., Peña, I., Pikman, M. and Ukon, M. 2009. *The 2009 BCG Multilatinas. A Fresh Look at Latin America and How a New Breed of Competitors Are Reshaping the Business Landscape*. Boston: The Boston Consulting Group.

Alden, C. and Hughes, C. R. 2009. Harmony and discord in China's Africa strategy: some implications for foreign policy. In J. Strauss and M. Saavedra (Eds), *China and Africa, Emerging Patterns of Globalisation and Development*. Cambridge: Cambridge University Press.

América Economía; Ranking Multilatinas 2011; http://rankings.americaeconomia.com/2011/multilatinas/ranking-multilatinas-completo.php; 20/4/2011.

Arnold, D. J. and Quelch, J. A. 1998. New strategies in emerging markets. *Sloan Management Review*, 40(1): 7.

Authers, J. 2006. The long view: how adventurous are emerging markets? *Financial Times*. 20/10/2006.

Barcena, A. and Rosales, O. 2010. *La República Popular China y América Latina y el Caribe: hacia una relación estratégica*. Santiago de Chile: ECLAC.

Barciela, F. 2011. Las 'multilatinas' devuelven la visita. *El País*. 16/1/2011.

BBC; South American nations found union; http://news.bbc.co.uk/2/hi/americas/7417896.stm; 16/4/2011.

BBC; Colombia country profile; http://news.bbc.co.uk/2/hi/americas/country_profiles/1212798.stm; 17/4/2011.

BBC; China country profile; http://news.bbc.co.uk/2/hi/asia-pacific/country_profiles/1287798.stm; 18/4/2011.

BBC Mundo; MERCOSUR/CAN: Libre Comercio; http://news.bbc.co.uk/hi/spanish/latin_america/newsid_3599000/3599535.stm; 16/4/2011.

Beattie, A. 2009. Argentina: the superpower that never was. *Financial Times*. 23/5/2009.

Best, E.; Supranational institutions and regional integration; www.eclac.org/brasil/noticias/paginas/2/22962/BEST <http://www.eclac.org/brasil/noticias/paginas/2/22962/BEST>; 20/4/2011.

Bin, S. 2006. The political economy of an Asian Pacific trade area: a China perspective, *An APEC Trade Agenda? The Political Economy of a Free Trade Area of the Asia Pacific*. Singapore: The Pacific Economic Cooperation Council/The APEC Business Advisory Board.

Blazquez-Lidoy, J., Rodriguez, J. and Santiso, J. 2006. *Angel or Devil? China's Trade Impact on Latin American Emerging Markets*. Paris: OECD Development Centre.

Boisot, M. and Child, J. 1996. From fiefs to clans and network capitalism: explaining China's emerging economic order. *Administrative Science Quarterly*, 41: 600–628.

Boisot, M. and Meyer, M. 2008. Which way through the open door? Reflections on the internationalization of chinese firms. *Management and Organization Review*, 4(3): 349–365.

Bravo, X. 2006. China se convirtió en noviembre en el mayor destino de envíos chilenos. *La Tercera*. 20/12/2006.

Brown, R. 1995. *Chinese Business Enterprise in Asia*. London: Routledge.

Buckley, P. and Casson, M. 1976. *The Future of the Multinational Enterprise*. London: Macmillan.

Buckley, P. and Ghauri, P. 1993. Introduction and overview. In P. Buckley and P. Ghauri (Eds), *The Internationalization of the Firm: A Reader*. London: Academic Press.

Buckley, P. and Casson, M. C. 1998. Analysing foreign market entry strategies: extending the internationalisation approach. *Journal of International Business Studies*, 29(3): 539–562.

Buckley, P., Clegg, J., Cross, A., Liu, X., Voss, H. and Zheng, P. 2007. The determinants of Chinese outward foreign direct investment. *Journal of International Business Studies*, 38(4): 499–518.

Butt-Philip, A. 2004. The great banana saga. *University of Bath School of Management case study – unpublished.*

Cai, K. 1999. Outward foreign direct investment: a novel dimension of China's integration into the regional and global economy. *China Quarterly* (160): 836–880.

CAN; Comunidad Andina de Naciones Official Site; http://www.comunidadandina.org/; 11/4/2011.

Cardoza, G. and Fornes, G. 2009. The Internationalisation of SMEs from China: the Case of Ningxia Hui Autonomous Region. *Asia Pacific Journal of Management*, DOI: 10.1007/s10490-009-9174-z.

Cardoza, G. and Fornes, G. 2011. National and International Expansion of Chinese SMEs. A Different Story? In X. Fu and W. Wu (Eds), *China's Role in Global Economic Recovery*. London: Routledge.

Cardoza, G., Fornes, G. and Xu, N. 2011. *Institutional determinants of Chinese SMEs' internationalization. The case of Jiangsu Province*. Paper presented at the Chinese Economic Association, Dublin.

CARICOM; CARICOM Official Site; http://www.caricom.org/; 16/4/2011.

Casanova, L. and Fraser, M. 2008. Introduction. In IADB (Ed.), *From Multilatinas to Global Latinas. The New Latin American Multinationals. (Compilation case studies)*. Washington: Inter-American Development Bank.

Casanova, L. and Hoeber, H. 2008. Pollo Campero – A Guatemala chicken flying across global borders. In IADB (Ed.), *From Multilatinas to Global Latinas. The New Latin American Multinationals. (Compilation case studies)*. Washington: Inter-American Development Bank.

Casanova, L. and Molina, R. 2008. Viña Concha y Toro – Chile's global wine. In IADB (Ed.), *From Multilatinas to Global Latinas. The New Latin American Multinationals. (Compilation case studies)*. Washington: Inter-American Development Bank.

Chantasasawat, B., Fung, K., Iizaka, H. and Siu, A. 2005. *FDI Flows to Latin America, East and Southeast Asia and China: Substitutes or Complements?* Japan: ADBi Publishing.

Chen, H. and Chen, T. 1998. Network linkages and location choice in foreign direct investment. *Journal of International Business Studies*, 29(3): 445–467.

Chen, J. 2006. Development of Chinese small and medium-sized enterprises. *Journal of Small Business and Enterprise Development*, 13(2): 140–147.

Child, J. and Tse, D. 2001. China's transition and its implications for international business. *Journal of International Business Studies*, 32: 5–21.

Child, J. and Rodrigues, S. 2005. The internationalization of Chinese firms: a case for theoretical extension? *Management and Organization Review*, 1(3): 381–410.

China Council for the Promotion of International Trade. 2010. *Survey on Current Conditions and Intention of Outbound Investment by Chinese Enterprises*. Beijing: China Council for the Promotion of International Trade.

China Daily; China, Chile sign free-trade agreement; http://www.chinadaily.com.cn/english/doc/2005–11/18/content_496004.htm; 18/4/2011.

China Development Bank; SMEs an Ever-growing Driver of Economic Growth; http://www.cdb.com.cn/English/NewsInfo.asp?NewsId=437; 1/2/2010.

CIA; The World Factbook – Costa Rica; https://www.cia.gov/library/publications/the-world-factbook/geos/cs.html; 20/4/2011.

CIA; The World Factbook – China; https://www.cia.gov/library/publications/the-world-factbook/geos/ch.html; 18/4/2011.

CIA. 2011c. *The World Factbook*. Washington D.C.: Central Intelligence Agency.

CIA; The World Factbook – Ecuador; https://www.cia.gov/library/publications/the-world-factbook/geos/ec.html; 204/2011.

CNN.com; Officials: G-20 to supplant G-8 as international economic council http://edition.cnn.com/2009/US/09/24/us.g.twenty.summit/index.html; 12/1/2011.

CNNExpansion.com; Cemex busca 'construir' negocio en China; http://www.cnnexpansion.com/negocios/2011/02/24/cemex-acciones-china-cemento-zambrano; 21/4/2011.

Costa, M. 2011. *Mercosur and the promise of develoment: trade associations stepping up to the challenge*. Paper presented at the IPSA-ECPR Conference Whatever happened to North-South?, Sao Paulo.

Cuervo-Cazurra, Á. 2002. Transforming the firm through co-evolution of resources and scope. In B. Chakravarthy and G. Mueller-Stewens and P. Lorange and C. Lechner (Eds), *Strategy Process: Shaping the Contours of the Field*. London: Blackwell.

Cuervo-Cazurra, Á. 2008. The multinationalization of developing country MNEs. The case of multilatinas. *Journal of International Management*, 14(2): 138–154.

Cuervo-Cazurra, Á. 2010. Multilatinas. *Universia Business Review*, Primer cuatrimestre: 14–33.

Dahlman, C. and Aubert, J.-E. 2001. *China and the Knowledge Economy: Seizing the 21st Century. WBI Development Studies*. Herndon: World Bank Publications.

Deutsche Bank; Depository Receipts Handbook; https://adr.db.com/drweb/public/en/docs/DepositaryReceiptsHandBook.pdf; 20/4/2011.

Deutsche Bank; DB Research; http://www.dbresearch.com/servlet/reweb2.ReWEB?rwnode=DBR_INTERNET_EN-PROD$RMLCHPM&rwsite=DBR_INTERNET_EN-PROD, 20/4/2011.

Dunning, J. 1977. Trade, location of economic activity, and the MNE: a search for an ecletic approach. In B. Ohlin and P. O. Hesselborn and P. M. Wijkman (Eds), *The International Allocation of Economic Activity*. London: Macmillan.

Dunning, J. 1995. Reappraising the eclectic paradigm in the age of alliance capitalism. *Journal of International Business Studies*, 26(3): 461–491.

Dunning, J. 1998. Location and the multinational enterprise: a neglected factor? *Journal of International Business Studies*, 26(1): 461–491.
Dussel Peters, E. 2005. *Economic opportunities and challenges posed by China for Mexico and Central America*. Bonn: DIE/GDI.
Dyer, G. and Lapper, R.; 2007. Pace of investments disappoints Latin America. *Financial Times*. 20/12/2007.
Dyer, G., Pilling, D. and Henny, S.; 2011. A strategy to straddle the planet. *Financial Times*. 17/1/2011.
ECLAC. 2005. *Latin America and the Caribbean in the World Economy 2004*. Santiago de Chile: Economic Commission for Latin America and the Caribbean.
ECLAC. 2006. *Foreign investment in Latin America and the Caribbean 2005*. Santiago de Chile: Economic Commission for Latin America and the Caribbean.
ECLAC. 2007. *Latin America and the Caribbean in the World Economy, 2006–2007*. Santiago de Chile: Economic Commission for Latin America and the Caribbean.
ECLAC. 2008. *Latin America and the Caribbean in the World Economy, 2007–2008*. Santiago de Chile: Economic Commission for Latin America and the Caribbean.
ECLAC. 2010a. *Foreign Direct Investment in Latin America and the Caribbean 2009*. Santiago: ECLAC.
ECLAC. 2010b. *Latin America and the Caribbean in the World economy. A crisis generated in the centre and a recovery driven by the emerging economies*. Santiago de Chile: ECLAC.
ECLAC. 2010c. Interactive Graphic System of International Trade Data; http://www.eclac.org/cgi-bin/getprod.asp?xml=/comercio/noticias/paginas/9/33539/P33539.xml&xsl=/comercio/tpl-i/p18f.xsl&base=/comercio/tpl-i/top-bottom.xsl; 15/1/2010.
ECLAC. 2010d. *Statistical Yearbook for Latin America and the Caribbean*. Santiago: Economic Commission for Latin America and the Caribbean.
ECLAC. 2011a. Interactive Graphic System of International Trade Data (SIGCI) – International Trade and Integration Division based on SITC Rev. 2. Santiago de Chile: ECLAC.
ECLAC. 2011b. *Foreign Direct Investment in Latin America and the Caribbean 2010*. Santiago: Economic Commission for Latin America and the Caribbean.
El Mundo; 2007. Alierta entra en el consejo de Netcom. *El Mundo*. 5/12/2007.
Embraer; 2002. Embraer sets up joint venture in China with AVIC II; http://www.embraer.com/en-US/ImprensaEventos/Press-releases/noticias/Pages/EMBRAER-FORMA-JOINT-VENTURE-COM-AVIC-II-NA-CHINA.aspx; 20/4/2011.
Esteban, M. 2009. The Chinese amigo: implications for the development of Equatorial Guinea. In J. Strauss and M. Saavedra (Eds), *China and Africa: Emerging Patterns in Globalisation and Development*. Cambridge: Cambridge University Press.
European Bank for Reconstruction and Development. 1998. *Transition Report 1998*. London: EBRD.
European Commission; www.europa.eu; 20/4/2011.
Eurostat. 2011. Total population.
Farzad, R.; 2007. Extreme investing: inside Colombia. *Business Week*. 28/5/2007.
Ferguson, N. 2011. The West and the rest: the changing global balance of power in historical perspective: Lecture at the Royal Institute of International Affairs,

London 9/5/2011, transcript available at www.chathamhouse.org.uk/publications/papers/view/-/id/1054/

Fernández Jilberto, A. and Hogenboom, B. 2010. Latin America and China. South-south relations in a new era. In A. Fernández Jilberto and B. Hogenboom (Eds), *Latin America Facing China. South-South Relations Beyond the Washington Consensus*. New York and Oxford: Berghahn Books.

Fornes, G. and Cardoza, G. 2007. Foreign Exchange Exposure in Emerging Markets. A study of Spanish companies in Latin America. *International Journal of Emerging Markets*, 3(3).

Fornes, G. 2008. *Foreign exchange exposure in emerging markets. A holistic approach to minimising its effects on multinational enterprises*. Paper presented at the Academy of Management Conference Best Paper Proceedings, Anaheim.

Fornes, G. and Butt-Philip, A. 2008. The growing relationship between China and Latin America, a source of opportunities? *Perspective*, Fall.

Fornes, G. 2009. *Foreign Exchange Exposure in Emerging Markets. How Companies Can Minimize It*. Basingstoke: Palgrave Macmillan.

Fornes, G. and Butt-Philip, A. 2009. Chinese companies' outward internationalisation to emerging countries: the Case of Latin America. *Chinese Business Review*, 7(1): 13–28.

Fornes, G. and Cardoza, G. 2009. Foreign exchange exposure in emerging markets. a study of Spanish companies in Latin America. *International Journal of Emerging Markets*, 4(1): 6–25.

Fornes, G. and Cardoza, G. 2010. Barriers and factors affecting the internationalisation of Chinese SMEs. In Y. Wang and P. Ramburuth (Eds), *Thirty Years of China's Economic Reform: Institutions, Management Organizations and Foreign Investment*. Hauppauge: Nova Science.

Fornes, G.; 2011. La importancia del eje China-Latinoamérica. *Cinco Días*. 12/4/2011.

Fornes, G. and Butt-Philip, A. 2011a. *Chinese MNCs in Latin America. An analysis of their characteristics and a comparison with their investments in developed countries*. Paper presented at the Chinese Economic Association, 2011.

Fornes, G. and Butt-Philip, A. 2011b. Chinese MNEs and Latin America. A review. *International Journal of Emerging Markets*, 6(2).

Fornes, G., Cardoza, G. and Xu, S. 2011. *The national and international expansion of SMEs from China. Evidence from Anhui Province*. Paper presented at the Academy of Management, San Antonio.

FTSE; FTSE Global Equity Index Series Country Classification; http://www.ftse.com/Indices/Country_Classification/Downloads/Sept%202010/FTSE_Country_Classification_Sept_2010_Update.pdf; 10/12/2010.

FTSE; Performance Analysis; http://www.ftse.com/Indices/FTSE_Emerging_Markets/Performance_Analysis.jsp; 14/1/2011.

Gallagher, K. 2010. Latin America must see China as a trade threat, as well as a partner. *Financial Times*. 11/11/2010.

Gallagher, K. and Porzecanski, R. 2010. *The Dragon in the Room. China and the Future of Latin American Industrialization*. Palo Alto: Stanford University Press.

Garcia-Herrero, A. and Santabarbara, D. 2005. Does China have an impact on foreign investment to Latin America? *China Economic Review*, 18(3): 266–286.

Ge, G. and Ding, D. 2008. A strategic analysis of sourcing Chinese manufacturers: the case of Galanz. *Asia Pacific Journal of Management*, 25(4): 667–683.

Goldman Sachs; Goldman Sachs Global Economics, Commodities and Strategy Research; http://www2.goldmansachs.com/ideas/brics/brics-decade-doc.pdf; 18/3/2011.

Gov.cn; Chinese Government's Official web portal; http://english.gov.cn/index.htm; 18/4/2011.

Gov.cn; Chinese Government's Official Web Portal – Official Publications; http://www.gov.cn/english/official/2008–11/05/content_1140347.htm; 20/4/2011.

Guthrie, D. 2005. Organizational learning and productivity: state structure and foreign investment in the rise of the Chinese corporation. *Management and Organization Review*, 1: 165–195.

Gutierrez, O. 2011. América Latina recela de la expansión de China. *El País*. 2/1/2011.

Haglund, D. 2009. Is it for the long run? Governance and learning among Chinese investors in Zambia's copper sector. In J. Strauss and M. Saavedra (Eds), *China and Africa: Emerging Patterns in Globalisation and Development*. Cambridge: Cambridge University Press.

Hoskisson, R. E., Eden, L., Lau, C. M. and Wright, M. 2000. Strategy in Emerging Economies. *Academy of Management Journal*, 43(3): 249–267.

House of Commons. 2007. Trade with Brazil and Mercosur. *Select Committee on Trade and Industry*, 1: 6.

Hughes, J. 2011. 'Bric' creator adds newcomers to list. *Financial Times*. 16/1/2011.

IADB. 2004. *The Emergence of China: Opportunities and Challenges for Latin America and the Caribbean*. Washington: Inter-American Development Bank.

International Finance Corporation. 1999. International Finance Corporation.

IMF; World Economic Outlook Database; http://www.imf.org/external/pubs/ft/weo/2010/02/weodata/index.aspx.

IMF; World Economic Outlook Database; http://www.imf.org/external/pubs/ft/weo/2011/01/weodata/index.aspx.

Independent Commission on International Development Issues and Brandt, W. 1980. *North-South, a Programme for Survival: Report of the Independent Commission on International Development Issues*. Cambridge: MIT Press.

Jenkins, R. 2008. *China's Global Growth and Latin American Exports*. Helsinki: UNU World Institute for Development Economics Research.

Jenkins, R., Dussel Peters, E. and Moreira, M. 2008. The impact of China on Latin America and the Caribbean. *World Development*, 36(2): 235–253.

Jiang, W. 2009. Fuelling the dragon: China's rise and its energy and resources extraction in Africa. In J. Strauss and M. Saavedra (Eds), *China and Africa: Emerging Patterns in Globalisation and Development*. Cambridge: Cambridge University Press.

Johanson, J. and Wiedersheim-Paul, F. 1975. The internationalization of the firm. Four Swedish cases. *Journal of Management Studies*, 12: 305–322.

Johanson, J. and Vahlne, J. 1977. The internationalization process of the firm. A model of knowledge development and increasing foreign market commitments. *Journal of International Business Studies*, 8: 23–32.

Khanna, T. and Palepu, K. 1997. Why focused strategies may be wrong for emerging markets. *Harvard Business Review*, 4(75): 3–10.

Khanna, T. and Palepu, K. 2000. The future of business groups in emerging markets: long-run evidence from Chile. *Academy of Management Journal*, 43(3): 268–285.

Khanna, T. and Palepu, K. 2002. Emerging giants: building world-class companies in emerging markets. *Harvard Business School Cases.*

Khanna, T. and Palepu, K. 2010. Multinationals in emerging markets. In T. Khanna and K. Palepu (Eds), *Winning in Emerging Markets: A Road Map for Strategy and Execution.* Boston: Harvard Business School Publishing Corporation.

Krauss, C. 2007. Latin American companies make big US gains. *New York Times.* 2/5/2007.

Kroll, L. and Miller, M.; 2010. The world's billionaires. *Forbes.* 3/10/2010.

Kumar, N. 1998. *Globalization, Foreign Direct Investment and Technology Transfers: Impacts on and Prospects for Developing Countries.* New York: Routledge.

La Nación. 2004a. Kichner y Hu Jintao firmaron convenios. *La Nación.* 16/11/2004.

La Nación. 2004b. Hu quiere una 'asociación estratégica'. *La Nación.* 18/11/2004.

La Nación. 2004c. China prometió que invertirá US$8000 millones en Brasil. *La Nación.* 16/11/2004.

La Nación. 2004d. China prevé invertir US$100.000 millones en América Latina. *La Nación.* 13/11/2004.

La Tercera. 2007a. Pekin estimulará la inversión exterior en cuatro sectores. *La Tercera.* 16–5–2007.

La Tercera. 2007b. China y Perú iniciarán conversaciones hacia TLC en los próximos días. *La Tercera.* 18/3/2007.

Lall, R. 2010. China provinces 'to be bigger than Russia'. *Financial Times.* 8/12/2010.

Lapper, R. 2005. Beijing's growing profile in Latin America. *Financial Times.* 9/3/2005.

Lapper, R. 2007. US agrees to China joining IADB. *Financial Times.* 18/3/2007.

Lapper, R. and Wheatley, J. 2008. Higher ground: Vale signals rise of 'multilatina'. *Financial Times.* 10/3/2008.

Large, D. 2009. China's Sudan engagement: changing Northern and Southern political trajectories in peace and war. In J. Strauss and M. Saavedra (Eds), *China and Africa: Emerging Patterns in Globalisation and Development.* Cambridge: Cambridge University Press.

Latibex; Latibex Official Site; http://www.latibex.com/; 26/4/2011.

Leahy, J. 2011a. Brazil looks to China for industrial Policy. *Financial Times.* 11/4/2011.

Leahy, J. 2011b. Brazil claims it is fifth largest economy in world. *Financial Times.* 3/3/2011.

Leahy, J. 2011c. Brazil and China trade tensions set to rise. *Financial Times.* 30/1/2011.

Leahy, J. 2011d. Brazilian factories tested by Chinese imports. *Financial Times.* 30/1/2011.

Lecraw, D. 1993. Outward direct investment by Indonesian firms: Motivation and effects. *Journal of International Business Studies,* 24: 589–600.

Leonidou, L. 2004. An analysis of the barriers hindering small business export development. *Journal of Small Business Management,* 42(3): 279–302.

Li, P., Fornes, G. and Cardoza, G. 2010. *The internationalisation of emerging markets-based SMEs: evidence from China's Shandong province.* Paper presented at the China Goes Global, Harvard University – Boston.

Li, P., Fornes, G. and Cardoza, G. 2010. The Internationalisation of emerging markets-based SMEs: evidence from China's Shandong province, *China Goes Global*. Harvard University – Boston.

Makino, S., Chung-Ming, L. and Rhy-Song, Y. 2002. Asset-exploitation versus asset-seeking: implications for location choice of foreign direct investment from newly industrialized economies. *Journal of International Business Studies*, 33(3): 403–421.

Malamud, A. 2007. The experience of European integration and the potential for integration in South America. *IBEI Working paper – Barcelona Institute of International Studies*: 15.

Malamud, A. 2008. The international agenda of Mercosur: interdependence, leadership, and institutionalisation. In G. Jaramillo (Ed.), *Los nuevos enfoques de la integracion, mas alla del regionalismo*. Quito: FLASCO.

Maloney, W. and Perry, G. 2005. Towards and efficient innovation policy in Latin America. *CEPAL Review*, 87: 25–43.

Marsh, P. 2011. Focus on deals high up value chain. *Financial Times*. 25/4/2011.

Mathews, J. 2006. Dragon multinationals: new players in 21st century globalization. *Asia Pacific Journal of Management*, 23(1): 5–27.

McGregor, R., Mitchell, T. and Dyer, G. 2006. China's biggest bank goes to market. *Financial Times*. 24/10/2006.

McGregor, R. 2011. Hu questions future role of US dollar. *Financial Times*. 16/1/2011.

Mercosur; Mercosur Official Site; www.mercosur.int; 11/4/2011.

Minda, A. 2008. The strategies of multilatinas: from the quest for regional leadership to the myth of the global corporation. *Cahiers du Gres*, 8(Mars 2008).

MOFCOM. 2007. *Statistical Bulletin of China's Outward Foreign Direct Investment*. Beijing: Ministry of Commerce the People's Republic of China.

MOFCOM. 2008. *Statistical Bulletin of China's Outward Foreign Direct Investment*. Beijing: Ministry of Commerce the People's Republic of China.

MOFCOM. 2009a. *Statistical Bulletin of China's Outward Foreign Direct Investment*. Beijing: Ministry of Commerce the People's Republic of China.

MOFCOM; China and Peru signed free trade agreement; http://fta.mofcom.gov.cn/enarticle/enperu/enperunews/200910/1215_1.html; 20/4/2011.

MOFCOM; China and Peru Signed Free Trade Agreement; http://english.mofcom.gov.cn/aarticle/newsrelease/significantnews/200905/20090506231332.html; 8/5/2009.

MOFCOM; China-Chile FTA on Service Trade Implemented; http://fta.mofcom.gov.cn/enarticle/enchile/enchilenews/201009/3501_1.html; 20/4/2011.

MOFCOM. 2010b. *Statistical Bulletin of China's Outward Foreign Direct Investment*. Beijing: Ministry of Commerce of China.

Mukhametdimov, M. 2007. Mercosur and the European Union: variation among the factors of regional cohesion. *Cooperation and Conflict*, 42: 201–225.

Naim, M. 2011. El crecimiento de América Latina depende de lo que pase en China. *El País*. 13/5/2011.

National Customs Service Gobierno de Chile; Chile-China Free Trade Agreement; http://www.aduana.cl/prontus_aduana_eng/site/artic/20070227/pags/20070227172530.html; 20/4/2011.

Nolan, P. 2001. *China and the Global Economy*. Basingstoke: Palgrave.

Omae, K. 1985. *Triad Power: the Coming Shape of Global Competition*. New York: Free Press.

Oxford Analytica 2010. 'Multilatinas' gain prominence. *Forbes*. 3/3/2010.

Painter, J. BBC News – Americas – China deepens Latin America ties; http://news.bbc.co.uk/go/pr/fr/-/2/hi/americas/7737554.stm; 23/11/2008.

Pang, E.-S. 2009. *Mercosur economic integration: lessons for ASEAN*. Singapore: ASEAN studies centre report #5 – Institute of South East Asian Studies – ISEAS Publishing.

Pearson, S. 2011a. China in talks with Brazil over trade barriers. *Financial Times*. 24/5/2011.

Pearson, S. 2011b. Brazil's carnival is 'made in China'. *Financial Times*. 6/3/2011.

Peng, M. 2003. Institutional transitions and strategic choices. *Academy of Management Review*, 28: 275–296.

Peng, M., Tan, J. and Tong, T. 2004. Ownership types and strategic groups in an emerging economy. *Journal of Management Studies*, 41: 1105–1129.

People's Daily Online; China signs free trade agreement with Costa Rica; http://english.peopledaily.com.cn/90001/90778/90861/6945374.html; 20/4/2011.

Phillips, T. 2010. Brazil's huge new port highlights China's drive into South America. *Guardian.co.uk*. 15/9/2010.

Porter, M. 1990. *The Competitive Advantage of Nations*. New York: Free Press.

Porter, M. 1998. Competing across locations: enhancing competitive advantage through a global strategy. In M. Porter (Ed), *On Competition*. Boston: Harvard Business School Press.

Quan, Y. 2001. Access to the WTO and internationalization strategy of Chinese companies. *Enterprise Studies*, 8: 12–24.

Rathbone, J. P. and Mapstone, N.; 2011. China in talks over Panama Canal rival. *Financial Times*. 13/2/2011.

Rauch, J. and Trindade, V. 2002. Ethnic Chinese networks in international trade. *The Review of Economics and Statistics*, February: 116–130.

Robledo, J.; La hora de las multilatinas; http://www.bbc.co.uk/mundo/noticias/2010/11/101125_multinacionales_latinas_espana_economia_amab.shtml; 20/4/2011.

Romei, V. and Wheatley, J. 2010. Brazil's shifting export structure. *Financial Times*. 1/11/2010.

Root, F. 1994. *Entry Strategies for International Markets*. San Francisco: Jossey-Bass.

Rovzar, A. 2009. Multilatinas: continued expansion. *Latin Business Chronicle*. 8/1/2009.

Rugman, A. and Li, J. 2007. Will China's multinationals succeed globally or regionally? *European Management Journal*, 25(5): 333–343.

Rui, H. and Yip, G. 2008. Foreign acquisitions by Chinese fSirms: a strategic intent perspective. *Journal of World Business*, 43(2): 213–226.

Saigol, L. and Thomas, H. 2010. Emerging markets M&A outstrips Europe. *Financial Times*. 19/9/2010.

Sanchez Ancochea, D. 2006. El impacto de China en América Latina: ¿oportunidad o amenaza? , *ARI – Real Instituto Elcano*, Vol. 38: 4–8.

Santiso, J. 2005a. America Latina y Asia: bailando con los tigres y los dragones asiaticos, *Anuario Elcano: America Latina 2004–2005*: 275–298.

Santiso, J. 2005b. La emergencia de China y su impacto en America Latina. *Politica Exterior*, 19(107): 97–112.

Santiso, J. 2006a. Of dragons & elephants, *LatinFinance*, Vol. September.

Santiso, J. 2006b. El triángulo China, España, y Latin América, *Percepciones – Centro de Desarrollo de la ODCE*, Vol. Setiembre.

Santiso, J. (Ed.). 2007. *The visible hand of China in Latin America*. Paris: OECD Development Centre Studies.

Schwab, K. 2006. *The Latin America Competitiveness Review 2006. Paving the Way for Regional Prosperity*. Geneva: World Economic Forun.

Sender, H. and Anderlini, J. 2011. CIC set for up to $200bn in fresh funds. *Financial Times*. 25/4/2011.

Shixue, J. 2007. *South-South Cooperation across the Pacific: Development of the Relations between China and Latin American*. Beijing: Chinese Academy of Social Sciences.

Shixue, J. How Can EU/Spain Help China Develop Its Relations with Latin America?; 27/4/2011.

Shoham, A. and Rosenboim, M. 2009. China's new approach to ODI in Africa: a model for a government seeking natural resources. In I. Alon and J. Chang and M. Fetscherin and C. Lattemann (Eds), *China Rules. Globalization and Political Transformation*. Basingstoke and New York: Palgrave Macmillan.

Solana Gonzalez, G. (Ed.). 2008. *China: Una necesidad para una empresa global*. Madrid: Universidad Antonio Nebrija.

Spar, D. and Oi, J. 2006. China: building 'capitalism with socialist characteristics'. *Harvard Business School Cases*, 9–706-041.

Sutherland, D. and Ning, L. 2011. Exploring 'onward-journey' ODI strategies in China's private sector business. *Journal of Chinese Economic and Business Studies*, 9(1): 43–65.

The Economist. 2008. Ins and Outs. Acronyms BRIC out all over. *The Economist*. 18/9/2008.

The Economist. 2010. How to stop a currency war. *The Economist*. 14/10/2010.

Tseng, W. 1994. The process of internationalisation of PRC multinationals. In H. Schultte (Ed.), *The Global Competitiveness of the Asian Firm*. Basingstoke: Macmillan.

UN. 2009a. *International Trade Statistics Yearbook – volume I trade by country*. New York: United Nations.

UN; World Urbanization Prospects. The 2009 Revision.; http://esa.un.org/unpd/wup/index.htm; 27/1/2011.

UNASUR; UNASUR Official Site; http://www.pptunasur.com/; 16/4/2011.

UNCTAD. 2006. *World Investment Report*. Geneva: United Nations.

UNCTAD. 2010. *World Investment Report*. Geneva: United Nations Conference on Trade and Development.

UNCTAD; UNCTADStat; http://unctadstat.unctad.org/TableViewer/tableView.aspx?ReportId=88; 18/1/2011.

UNData; Composition of macro geographical (continental) regions, geographical sub-regions, and selected economic and other groupings; http://unstats.un.org/unsd/methods/m49/m49regin.htm.

UNDP; Human Development Report.

Warner, M., Ng, S.-H. and Xu, X. 2004. 'Late development' experience and the evolution of transnational firms in the People's Republic of China. *Asia Pacific Business Review*, 10: 324–345.

Webb, T. 2010. World gripped by 'international currency war'. *The Guardian*. 28/9/2010.

Wells, L. 1981. Foreign investors from the Third World. In K. Kumar and M. McLeod (Eds), *Multinational from developing countries*: 23–36. Lexington, MA: Health and Company.

Wells, L. 1983. *Third World Multinationals: The Rise of Foreign Direct Investment from Developing Countries*. Cambridge, MA: MIT Press.

Williamson, P. and Yin, E. 2009. Racing with the Chinese dragons. In I. Alon and J. Chang and M. Fetscherin and C. Lattemann (Eds), *China Rules. Globalization and Political Transformation*: 69–100. Basingstoke and New York: Palgrave Macmillan.

Wolf, M. 2011. Europe should not control the IMF. *Financial Times*. 24/5/2011.

Wong, J. and Chan, S. 2003. China's outward direct investment: expanding worldwide. *China: An International Journal*, 1(2 (Sep. 2003)): 273–301.

Wright, M., Filatotchev, I., Hoskisson, R. E. and Peng, M. W. 2005. Strategy research in emerging economies: challenging the conventional wisdom. *Journal of Management Studies*, 42(1): 1–33.

WTO. 2000. *International Trade Statistics*. Geneva: World Trade Organisation.

WTO. 2006. *World Trade Report*. Geneva: World Trade Organisation.

WTO. 2008. *World Trade Report*. Geneva: World Trade Organization.

WTO. 2009. Lamy hails accord ending long running banana dispute: Press release 15/12/2009.

WTO. 2010a. *Participation of Developing Economies in the Global Trading System*. Geneva: World Trade Organisation.

WTO. 2010b. *International Trade Statistics*. Geneva: World Trade Organisation.

Xiong, C. 2011. Que espera China de España en su acercamiento a Latino América?: Lecture at ESIC Business and Marketing School, Madrid, Spain, 2/6/2011.

Xu, N., Fornes, G. and Cardoza, G. 2009. *The Internationalisation of Emerging Markets-based SMEs: Evidence from China's Jiangsu Province*. Paper presented at the China Goes Global Conference, Harvard University – Boston.

Xu, S., Fornes, G. and Cardoza, G. 2010. *The Internationalisation of Emerging Markets-based SMEs: Evidence from China's Anhui Province*. Paper presented at the Chinese Economic Association Conference, Oxford.

Yamakawa, Y., Peng, M. and Deeds, D. 2008. What drives new ventures to internationalize from emerging to developed economies? *Entrepreneurship Theory and Practice*, 32(1): 59–82.

Yeung, H. and Olds, K. (Eds). 2000. *Globalization of Chinese business firms*. New York: St Martin's Press.

Zeng, M. and Williamson, J. 2003. The hidden dragons *Harvard Business Review*, October 2003: 92–99.

Zeng, M. and Williamson, P. 2007. *Dragos at Your Door: How Chinese Cost Innovation Is Disrupting Global Competition*. Boston, MA: Harvard Business School Press.

Zhang, J. and Van Den Bulcke, D. 1996. International management strategies of Chinese multinational firms. In J. Child and Y. Lu (Eds), *Management Issues in China: International Enterprises*. London: Routledge.

Zhiming, Z. 2010. *Inside the Growth Engine. a Guide to China's Regions, Provinces, and Cities* Hong Kong: HSBC.

Index